Housing, Rural Poor and Their Living Conditions

C. PARVATHAMMA
SATYANARAYANA

Gian Publishing House
29/6 SHAKTI NAGAR • DELHI-110007 • INDIA

GIAN PUBLISHING HOUSE
29/6, SHAKTI NAGAR, DELHI - 110007

ISBN 81-212-0088-1

PRINTED IN INDIA

Published by Mrs. Gayatri Garg for Gian Publishing House, Delhi-110007 and Printed by Shri Dhar Bhatt for Kalyani Printers (Composing Unit), Delhi-110035

Acknowledgements

I thank the Government of Karnataka in particular Dr. D. M. Nanjundappa, Secretary to the Government, Planning Department, for having provided the funds to carry out a research project in 1987.

The implementation of the study was delayed due to unforeseen circumstances. We made a slow beginning and the data collection in Mysore and Bangalore Revenue Divisions of the state was completed by the research staff during 1979.

Despite some delay I am happy that the work has come to a successful end. We hope the findings would be of practical use to the policy makers. Incidentally the purpose of initiating the present study itself was intended to be evaluative, thereby indicating that the findings would not be put in cold storage.

I wish to record my thanks to the various known and unknown officers who have helped to carryout field-work and have supplied preliminary information. I also thank the innumerable respondents; the houseless, those living in *Janata* houses and others. The work carried out by the Research staff sometimes amidst adverse conditions particularly in the field situation is appreciated.

I am thankful to Sri Satyanarayana who evinced interest in the present study from the stage of writing the report hence, I invited him to be coauthor of the work.

Sri R. Nagaraj, helped by typing the script and I record my thanks to him for the timely help. To Messrs Gian Publishing House Delhi, I am very thankful for having broughtout the book in record time.

C. PARVATHAMMA

Professor & Head
Department of Sociology,
University of Mysore,
Mysore-6

List of Tables

Contents

1

Introduction

MEN LIVE in a world which poses many threats to their security. The cultures that men create represent ways of adopting to these threats to security. Housing, as an element of material culture is one such device to overcome threats against physical or security to life and serves an important purpose by making the provisions of shelter. It provides a place for the operation of many human activities. House serves the common purposes like feeding the members, working, sleeping, child-rearing, entertaining, leisure and many more activities.[1] Irrespective of space and time, man is using a place of accommodation which we call it as a house. It helps people to interact within the family and with outside world.

One of the usual questions raised in the evaluation of housing is how adequately it shelters individuals from threats in their environment ? The cultural history of humanity looked towards house as a place of safety from both non-human and human threats. Almost every person is affected in his day-to-day living by the kind of house in which he lives. Many people—particularly housewives, children and elders—spend most of the time in the

1. Hartman W. Chester : 1975, *Housing and Social Policy,* Prentice Hall Inc. USA, p. 3.

home than in any other single place. Therefore, house becomes the place where individuals can exercise maximum autonomy. Moreover, house acquires a sacred character from its complex intertwining with the self and from the symbolic character it has as a representation of the family. Consequently, the nature of the space is an important determinant of personal and family satisfaction.

It is partinent to know what a house is or what is meant by housing ? Beyer (1965) concluded it as a bulky, durable and permanent product which has a fixed location being used only in the place where it is built. Once built it tends to remain in existence for many years—frequently long after it has served its usefulness. It becomes almost a part of the land.[2] However, Eyheralde (1960) differentiated physical house from cultural home. Cultural house is what we call the family—one of the social institutions. The controversy between the physical and cultural house remains unresolved. But when Mumford (1938) remarks that the dwelling place is building arranged in such a fashion that food may be easily prepared, served and stored, that the processes of hygiene and sanitation facilitated, that rest and sleep may be enjoyed without disturbance from the outside world and that the care of young may be carried on under favourable conditions of companionship and supervision that the convincing social definition of house or home is arrived at.

These days priority is given to find out a house at least with basic conveniences. Importance is given not only to the dwelling place but also to surroundings. Therefore, housing includes far more than living space and shelter. Its nature and value are determined by the facilities it gives. These facilities are many including neighbourhood facilities, access to education, health amenities and security.[3]

Under the changing trend of housing, many people feel that their living conditions are very important. Many countries in the

---

2. Beyer : 1965, *Housing and Society*, Macmillan, New York, p. 3.

3. Grimes F. Orville : 1976, *Housing for Low Income Urban Families*, John Hopkins University Press, Baltimore, p. 25.

world have been viewing housing as not only as individuals' concern but a social one. The housing policies and programmes of different nations reflect the social aspect of the housing. For Hartman (1975), housing conditions should be understood to include not only the physical conditions of the dwelling unit but control over living conditions, the cost of housing in relation to perceived value and ability to afford these costs, the conditions of the surrounding neighbourhood, social life, and accessibility to community facilities and employment.[4]

Thus the availability and the kind of social, medical facilities, jobs, shopping and transportation facilities influence housing. Housing conditions then design the individual's place in the society and the country's progress at large. In this sense th' housing conditions should consist of both the physical and social contexts which would naturally reflect the living conditions of the people.

The housing conditions may vary in accordance with the needs of the people since the general standard to set housing conditions differs from country to country. Hence, each country has set forth certain minimum conditions regarding housing.

Cullingworth (1960) writes that when people lack or are deprived of most of the specified standards of housing conditions, there is a housing-need. The inadequacy of the existing facilities and provisions will create the housing-need among the people. Today people all over the world face the housing need much more than the housing supply. They accommodate themselves somehow though the lack of basic housing amenities causes serious discomforts.

A U.N. working group on housing and building materials explain that the chronic shortage of housing is seen mainly among the lower income groups and among the poor people. As is natural, there is a tendency among these groups to build houses of the lowest standard. The poor are satisfied if they get just a

4. Hartman, W.C.: 1975, *Housing and Social Policy*, Prentice Hall, USA, p. 3.

small place to sleep and do not bother about the other facilities not to speak of standard housing conditions.[5]

Nevertheless, housing needs in any country can be measured along a number of dimensions such as the physical quality of the dwelling unit, extent of overcrowding, the burden of housing costs and the quality of the social and physical environment.

Some of the urgent remedies that could be suggested to reduce the problems of housing are to cut down the costs of new construction and to provide at least the basic amenities. These can solve the people's deprivation or needs for housing.

In the estimation of housing needs, present and future, two variables have to be taken into account :

(*i*) the population that has to be housed, and
(*ii*) the standard at which it has to be housed.

Housing—A World Picture

Though a house "corner of one's own" should be a human right, number of countries in the world are still hesitating the people's claim to a safe roof, shelter against the cold of the night, the heat of the day, the rain and the snow or bad weather.[6]

Of the fundamental human needs, food, clothing, health and shelter, the last item has traditionally ranked lowest in the priorities of most developing countries.[7]

Housing is included only as a 'package' right—the right to a standard of living adequate for health—including food, clothing, housing, medical care and social services vide Art. 25 of the Universal Declaration of Human Rights decades ago. It is not only an 'adequate standard of living' but includes both physical needs like schools, hospitals, roads, water supply and cultural needs of family well being.

World's population trend in 1970 has shown that out of

5. ECAFE, 1960, Bangkok, p. 44.
6. Arnold, A. : *A place to live*, Allied Publishers, Bombay, p. 5.
7. Steedman David W. : 1979, *Housing Asia's Millions*, International Development Research Centre, Canada, p. 7.

about 365 crores, 65 per cent lived in rural areas. It is estimated that by the end of the century, the ratio of rural-urban population may be almost equal of 50 : 50. The process of urbanward migration, natural increase of city population due to population growth have influenced continued deterioration of housing conditions in the world. The other factor which aggravated the sorry state of affairs of housing is inadequate allocation of resources. Under this category are included the rural population who are generally very much neglected.

The situation is quite alarming when many countries are building only 3 to 4 dwelling units per 100 people. The UN report for the Second Development Decade estimated 8 to 10 units. This means there is huge deficit of housing units leading to overcrowding in many countries while sanitary conditions and water supply lag far behind.[8]

Now a number of countries have adopted housing and building policies. Many have had housing census. It was also realised by some of the industrialised countries that housing and building are generators of economic development in terms of investment and employment. Some of them have invested 4 per cent of their GNP. France, for instance, invests 6 per cent. But what is not encouraging to the poor is that there has been too much emphasis on luxury housing and this has caused greater inequalities in societies that are not centrally planned.

In India, information on housing conditions in rural areas is very scanty and difficult to collect. Both land owners and government are not showing interest to improve housing conditions in the villages. This is unfortunate as the nation's foreign exchange earnings often come from the exports of agricultural commodities from rural areas of which very little is invested to bring about improvement in conditions of rural life.

Housing poses a different problem in the rural areas. There is the need for better quality housing and facilities. Present rural

8. 'World Housing Survey' 1973 UN Committee on Housing, Building and Planning E/C6/129.

houses are by and large built mostly with non-durable materials. Generally the most immediate housing needs are those brought about by the rapid growth of urban centres. On the other hand, very rarely housing problem in the rural areas has attracted attention of planners. Often it is viewed that rural housing is suited to the climate, environment and traditional social structure. But a close look at rural housing reveals how sub-standard they are by the present social and legal norms.

Besides, the problem of those unfortunate people who have no roof to sleep under has been completely ignored. Some countries might have paid special attention to the problem of the houseless. But largely these are concerned with instances of natural disasters and war devastations. Other schemes may be related to the needs arising from a refugee situation or as a consequence of public works like construction of dam, hospital, etc. A great deal of action is yet to be initiated in fulfilling that basic human right—a corner of one's own—in many developing societies.

Methodology

The present study refers to the problems of the houseless and their living conditions and housing in general in rural Karnataka. The project was financed by the Government of Karnataka. It covers eleven[9] districts of two revenue sub-divisions (Bangalore and Mysore) in the State. Besides the rural houseless, the study also includes an evaluation of the *Janata* Housing (People Housing) scheme implemented in different phases by the State Government. A comparative analysis of the living conditions of people other than the above two groups is also attempted. Thus the study covers three groups of people in villages in relation to housing in each of the eleven districts :

(*i*) The houseless people.
(*ii*) Those living in *Janata* houses.
(*iii*) People living in other types of houses.

9. Bangalore, Chikmagalur, Chitradurga, Coorg, Hassan, Kolar, Mandya, Mysore, Shimoga, South Kanara and Tumkur.

The department of Post-graduate studies and research in Sociology, University of Mysore, was entrusted with this work. The background of the study reported here and the objectives with which it was undertaken can be stated as under :

> The Planning Department of the Government of Karnataka wanted to have an objective assessment of the magnitude of the problems of houseless people in villages. On enquiry, the department of Sociology, Mysore University, proposed to undertake a research study to find out the existing housing conditions and their social relevance in villages in Karnataka with special reference to the poor and the houseless. Through an empirical study it was intended to map out those who do not have adequate or no dwelling places of their own, the reasons, its impact on the basic social life of people, and possible remedies. The study also included reaction of different sections of people in the village to various schemes provided for the benefit of the poor.

Some of the main objectives of the research study to

(1) identify the poor in rural areas ;
(2) assess the housing pattern in relation to economic and social structure of the village ;
(3) understand the difference in living conditions of houseless people within the village, between villages and districts in the state ;
(4) highlight the differences observed between developed, developing and underdeveloped areas ;
(5) find out who are the beneficiaries of governmental schemes regarding distribution of the house sites, and other benefits connected with housing ;
(6) examine the meaning of *pucca* and *kuchcha* houses in villages and the structural variations ;
(7) evaluate the *Janata* housing programme in rural Karnataka.

On the whole it was very important to know the effective role played by government schemes in meeting the present demand. This would help formulating future policies by the state government.

Design and Implementation of the Study

To start with the research programme required certain basic information such as number of villages in the two revenue sub-divisions. Also it was necessary to get details of number of people who are houseless in the state and in the two sub-divisions.

Data connected with various schemes of rural housing have to be obtained from government departments. Further, it was necessary to know the areas which are relatively developed or otherwise in the state. Therefore, these details had to be obtained from various agencies concerned.

Apart from the secondary data mentioned, the study also sought some basic demographic information such as age, sex, marital status, education, occupation, annual income and expenditure of the household members separately for the houseless, *Janata* and other groups in the village. The survey also sought to obtain some information regarding the type of houses viz., *kuchcha*, *pucca* in which people are living as the ownership pattern, people's assessment of housing problem in the village, knowledge of government assistance, desirability of separate housing for each caste, sub-caste, consequences of mixed housing colony and so forth. The study envisaged to ascertain the economic conditions of the three groups—houseless, those residing in *Janata* houses and others—in relation to their possessions, both movables and immovables. The attitude of people about the village panchayat, co-operatives and their assessment of panchayats and panchayat members' role in the development of the village is included.

The study sought to know from those who are living in *Janata* houses, how they came to know the scheme, who helped them to get the benefit, the role of middlemen, suitability of the house in relation to their present needs, basic facilities provided to them and their neighbourhood.

The empirical data containing details of number of houseless people in the village, their present position, period and reasons for not owning a house, their comprehension about being houseless in the village have also been assessed.

The research study sought to know the opinion of the rural rich on the implementation of *people housing scheme.*

Finally, the survey attempted to find out the relation between land and the social conditions of people in villages. Information was sought to understand villagers' opinion regarding changing pattern in land-holding, distribution of land to landless, desirability of owning land, success in cultivation. It sought to find out the role of land tribunals in solving the problem of the rural poor.

Sample

As explained earlier, the study is formulated on a multi-stage sample. The state has 19 districts divided into 4 administrative sub-divisions. They are :

1. Bangalore — Covering the districts of Bangalore : Tumkur — Kolar — Chitradurga and Shimoga.
2. Mysore — Including the districts of Mysore : Mandya — Hassan — Coorg — Chikmagalur and South Kanara.
3. Belgaum — Comprising the districts of Belgaum : Dharwar — Bijapur and North Kanara.
4. Gulbarga — Comprising the districts of Gulbarga : Bidar — Raichur and Bellary.

All the eleven districts in Bangalore and Mysore revenue divisions are included in the study. Out of 94 taluks in the two divisions, 50 were selected giving equal weightage to the developed and underdeveloped taluks.

While selecting 100 villages—two from each of the 50 selected taluks—the following aspects were kept in view.

(1) Villages which have large areas of dry lands,

(2) Villages which have large areas of wet lands,

(3) Nearness of otherwise to main roads, and

(4) Villages where the *Janata* housing scheme is implemented.

All taluks where the district headquarters are located are selected automatically;

Thirty households from each selected village are included in the study out of which fifteen are *Janata* houses. The remaining 15 would be houseless families. In the event these numbers are not available in any sample village, other houses such as *kuchcha*[10] and *pucca*[11] are included.

On the whole details of 2924 households are covered in the study.

Problems of Sampling

When the sample was being drawn in early 1979 the state government was approached for certain basic data regarding various housing schemes in the state, estimated number of houses constructed, work-in-progress and proposed construction and so forth. The government departments informed that the updated figures are not readily available. Similarly, there was no source to get the number of houseless population in the state. The problem got further complicated since the study was designed to give due weightage to the developed and developing taluks.

There was no single source to identify taluks which are developed or otherwise. Therefore, it involved a lot of work to compile the data drawn from the statistical abstracts of the state relating to 1971 census.

Again, details were not readily available regarding villages which have predominantly wet or dry lands. It was rather difficult

10. Houses constructed with non-durable material like grass, leaves, reeds, bamboo, thatch and mud.

11. Houses constructed with durable material.

to select sample villages keeping in view the road communicatino to the villages in the absence of proper road maps of the state including villages.

Data indicating the number of *janata* houses constructed in each village was not available. In spite of repeated requests, many of the Block Development Officers (BDO) in the selected taluks did not respond to the request.

In view of the difficulties explained, after selecting taluks, the research staff went to taluk headquarters to obtain details of housing schemes before proceeding to particular villages. As usual, many Block Development Officers did not co-operate with the research group. Several BDOs were either not available for a number of days in their offices or the office staff pleaded their inability to give any information regarding housing schemes coming under their jurisdiction.

Interview Guide

An interview guide was prepared by the project staff in consultation with the project director. The English version was translated to Kannada. While translating, care was taken to retain the meaning of question rather than literal transcription. Sophisticated and literary words were avoided.

The interview guide is divided into four major parts. The *first part* contains household details such as identification of the respondents, personal information of members of the household. Questions onthe housing problem, respondents' membership in village cooperative society, their opinion on the role of village panchayat and land reforms are included here.

The *second part* consists of questions relating to *janata* housing scheme, facilities provided in them and so forth.

The *third part* includes questions on housing problems faced by the houseless people, their living conditions and the reasons for remaining without house.

The *final part* concerns questions that would give the opinion of the rural rich on the *janata* housing scheme.

Thus the four parts are divided among different categories of respondents to highlight the problems at various levels. On the whole, the questions cover the major objectives of this study.

Pilot Study

A pilot study was conducted by the two Research Assistants in two villages near Mysore city. This helped framing the structured interview-guide which was further tested. The modified interview guide was printed before going for field work in selected villages.

After the printing of interview guides, field work was taken up by the two research assistants in the project. Districts which usually have heavy rains were covered first before the onset of monsoon. The remaining areas were taken up in succession. It took about 8 months to complete data-collection work.

Problems of Interviewing

When the investigators visited the houses, the respondents were often not readily available. Since most of them (respondents) are agricultural labourers and menial workers, usually they were at work-spot. After work they come back exhausted by night and it was very difficult to meet them. The research staff waited and where necessary stayed on to complete the interview and recorded information given by them.

Ignorance of government schemes, coupled with illiteracy of the respondents made the investigators to spend more time to explain certain facts in detail. Therefore, there was delay in getting the data.

Data Processing

When the proposal for the research study was given to the government, no provision was made in the budget estimates for mechanical tabulation. Therefore, manual tabulation procedure has to be adopted to process the data. But the sample size was relatively large. There were about 120 items in the interview guide and the number of households came upto 3000. As and when the research staff came after each round of field work, they were asked to edit the interview guides and to clear all doubts in recording appropriate information before they are taken up for tabulation.

Simultaneously, a code book was prepared and tested. Work on coding of responses, entry in the code cards and preparation of frequency tables was entrusted to two piece-rate research staff. It took nearly 10 months to complete the tabulation work. Inferences are drawn from the answers only by using simple tables. Also percentages are used to explain them in a simplified way.

Implementation of the Project and Recruitment of the Staff

The state government conveyed its approval for the study in June 1978 and informed the project director and the University of Mysore accordingly. But it took three months for the university to communicate the approval in spite of repeated reminders. The planning department, Government of Karnataka, was prompt in clarifying certain points raised by the Director of the study. Further the staff proposals sent by the Director of the project were held up without any reason for months in the university office. Even as the staff were recruited, for months together they were not paid their salary. On more than one occasion the morale of the staff was low because of the non-co-operation of the university administration.

Unnecessary protracted correspondence with the university office resulted in the stoppage of project work twice during the period of 18 months. The project director had to take decision pending sanction by the university to pay the salary of the staff because the administration refused to act even after months.

I record here the scant encouragement given to the researchers in the University centre. The big brother attitude of the executives in the university stalled the enthusiasm of the academicians. If research has to become meaningful, it requires a helpful administration within the existing framework of rules. Officials who hardly know A, B, C of research should not be allowed to sleep over papers and go scot free. But this is happening endlessly in our universities both to the detriment of academicians and the institutions. Instead of 'lay' administrators, it should be persons with research experience who hold charge of clearing research projects, problems and its administration.

Time Schedule

Initially the study was expected to be completed within 18 months. Because of the reasons stated above the project work had to be suspended twice. Hence the study took quite a few months more than expected.

2

Housing in India

PROVISIONS FOR adequate housing to the people is a complex problem. Many developing countries in the world including India unfortunately have given least priority for housing. Though the Indian Constitution lays down certain principles to provide basic socio-economic necessities like food, clothing and shelter, the conditions of millions are yet to improve.

Housing conditions both in urban and rural India are extremely unsatisfactory. Besides, there is acute shortage of houses and much of the available accommodation in urban areas is sub-standard. The reasons are very many. Rapid growth of population, continuous migration from rural areas, limited land, haphazard growth of cities and towns, increasing number of urban poor, steep rise in cost of construction-material and land, have all contributed to the present problem.

The situation in the rural areas is no better. Unlike urban house the concept of housing in rural India is different. The house is the physical environment in which the peasant family combines the simple social, cultural and physical aspects of their life. In that house children are born and bred, marriages are performed, visitors are entertained, rests and sleeps are forthcoming, artisans do their work, meals are prepared, goods are stored and domestic animals and cattle are kept.

Details of "Census of India : Classification of Household, 1961-71" are given in Table 1. A point has been raised with regard to shortage of houses in the village. The impression that every village family has got the benefit of a shelter is wrong. The fact that majority of the rural houses are single-roomed, there is no private yard, and families live very congested. This means housing shortage.

The shortage of houses is aggravated by the increase in rural population. Statements showing the growth of population between 1951-71 and the estimated housing demand, supply and shortage owing to population growth are given in Tables 2 and 3. The problems of floods and fire have also contributed to this. The shortage is on the increase because of dilapidation of the houses. It is well known that village houses are built with mud and thatch. Due to lack of skill, insufficient foundation and projection, the structure is gradually destroyed by the action of rains, winds and floods.

In 1971 there were about 9.3 crore dwelling units in India in which about 10.5 crore households lived. Out of these about 8.1 crores housing units were considered usable *pucca*, *semi-pucca* and serviceable *kachcha* houses. The shortage worked out to be 2.4 crore dwelling units. This accounted for 0.55 crore in urban areas and 1.85 crores in rural areas. Further, the annual shortage is estimated at 20 lakh units due to the growth of population.[1]

The National Sample Survey Reports contained data on housing conditions and related facilities such as the number of rooms occupied, the space, type of structure, sources of drinking-water, bath-rooms and so forth. Details for rural areas have shown that about 34 per cent households had only one room, while another 32 per cent had two rooms. Nearly 15 per cent had three rooms and about 19 per cent with four rooms and above. As many as 61 per cent of houses had plinths, walls and roofs of mud. The average per capita floor space worked to 59.5 sq. ft. and about

---

1. Chandramouli, M. : 'Housing in India—an Overview' in *A Place to Live*, Allied Publishers, Bombay, p. 19.

TABLE 1

Census of India
Classification of Household, 1961 to 1971
(in millions)

Types of houses or dwelling units	*1961*			*1971*			*1981*		
	Total	*Rural*	*Urban*	*Total*	*Rural*	*Urban*	*Total*	*Rural*	*Urban*
Dwelling units	77.22	63.64	13.58	89.66	71.93	17.73	103.14	80.94	22.20
Shop-cum-houses	0.67	0.44	0.23	1.06	0.79	0.27	1.17	0.88	0.29
Workshop-cum-houses	1.33	1.08	0.25	1.74	1.33	0.41	1.93	1.48	0.45
Total	79.22	65.16	14.06	92.46	74.05	18.41	106.24	83.30	22.94

Notes : 1. The housing stocks of 1961 and 1971 have been obtained from the office of Census Commissioner, Census of India, New Delhi.

2. 1981 figures have been estimated on the basis of trend rate of 1961 to 1971.

Source : Sinha B. D. Housing growth in India, Arnold-Heinemann, New Delhi, 1976, p. 120.

TABLE 2

Estimated Housing Shortage Owing to Population Growth and Replacement Requirement : 1951 to 1971
(in millions)

Year	Total			Rural			Urban		
	Due to growth	*Replace-ment*	*Total*	*Due to growth*	*Replace-ment*	*Total*	*Due to growth*	*Replace-ment*	*Total*
1951	7.858	2.307	10.165	5.663	2.028	7.691	2.195	0.279	2·474
1956	9.592	3.363	12.955	7.196	2.962	10.158	2.396	0.401	2.797
1961	8.612	4.676	13.288	6.900	4.079	10.979	1.712	0.597	2.309
1966	13.041	5.813	18.854	10.422	5.064	15.486	2.619	0.749	3.368
1971	17.122	7.268	24.390	13.895	6.291	20.186	3.227	0.977	4.204

Note : Replacement requirement have been estimated on the basis of NSS data—19th Round Report No. 195, pp. 4 and 5.

Source : B. D. Sinha (1976).

TABLE 3

Estimated Housing Demand, Supply and Shortage owing to Population Growth : 1951 to 1971
(in millions)

Year	Total			Rural			Urban		
	Demand	*Supply*	*Shortage*	*Demand*	*Supply*	*Shortage*	*Demand*	*Supply*	*Shortage*
1951	72.220	64.362	7.858	59.720	54 057	5.663	12.500	10.305	2.195
1956	79.720	70.128	9.592	65.560	58.364	7.196	14.160	11.764	2.396
1961	87.840	79.223	8.617	72.060	65.160	6.900	15.780	14.063	1.717
1966	98.220	85.179	13.041	79.580	69.158	10.422	18.640	16.021	2.619
1971	109.580	92.458	17.122	87.940	74.045	13.895	21.640	18.413	3.227

Note : Demand estimated yearwise on the basis of one house/dwelling unit for five persons. Population figures obtained from Census Reports. Supply of housing stock obtained for 1951, 1961 and 1971 from Census Reports, 1956 and 1966 figures were estimated on the basis of census data.

Source : Sinha, B.D. (1976), p. 118.

14.3 per cent households have a per capita floor space of 50 sq. ft. each or less. On the whole less than 0.5 per cent households have tap water. Roads, drainage, bathrooms, electricity and other facilities are not available to the village people. Wherever they are available the percentage is negligible.[2]

The houseless in India, it is estimated, were 12.65 lakhs. Among them 2.96 lakhs (23.4 per cent) lived in urban areas and 9.70 lakhs (76.6 per cent) lived in the rural areas. In some of our big cities, there are thousands of people who live on the pavements with their families.

The country in 1981 had 680 million population. In rural areas where 80 per cent of its population live in nearly 5.5 lakh villages, the housing conditions are very bad. One estimate has put the requirement of houses in rural areas at 80-90 million new units.

Only a small number of houses in rural India are *pucca* built with durable materials. While a large majority are either completely *kachcha* built with non-durable materials, or are partly *pucca* and partly *kachcha.* Details of rural house structure is given in Table 4. These non-durable houses need constant repairs and it is a strain on the villager, both financially and otherwise. According to 1971 census, nearly 50 per cent of the households do not have more than one room, some of them not even have a regular room at all. However, the number of persons living in a room is put at 5.3, which is very high.

The present position of housing statistics is unsatisfactory in relation to the needs of planning. Except for the details enumerated in decennial census, no other source provided information like the current building activities, additions made each year to existing houses, quantity and cost of material used, production and consumption of materials by building industry and so forth.

---

2. National Sample Survey Report Nos. 26, 50, 51, 67, 150, 165 and 174.

TABLE 4

Distribution of Census Houses in Rural India in 1971, by Predominant Material of Wall and Predominant Material of Roof

Total Number of Census Houses 98,417,376

Predominant Material of Wall			*Predominant Material of Roof*	
Grass, leaves, reeds or bamboo		11,380,127	Grass, leaves, reeds, thatch wood, mud, unburnt bricks or bamboo	49,607,189
Mud	—	47,919,453	Tiles, slate, shingle	36,552,860
Unburnt bricks	—	8,220,635	Corrugated iron, zinc or other metal sheets	4,799,325
Wood	—	1,289,334		
Burnt Bricks	—	15,306,827	Asbestos cement sheets	395,886
G. I. Sheets or other metal	—	139,294	Brick and Lime	1,492,249
Stone	—	13,939,552	Stone	2,609,524
Cement Concrete	—	131,570	Concrete, RBC/RCC	2,884,509
All other materials and materials not stated	—	90,584	All other materials and materials not stated	75,834

Source : Census of India, 1971 Series 1, Part VI-B, Housing. Tables as given in *Housing conditions in rural India*—S. K. Chandhoke, "IIC Quarterly", Vol. 4, No. 2, 1977, p. 182.

This work was completed at a time of considerable crisis and confusion on the Indian housing scene. General inflation in the economy has brought in major set-back. Government assistance dried up, minimised interest rates are higher and prices and cost of construction material rose steeply. The result is house construction falls, prices and rents are not within the reach of most families.

Housing shortage in rural India is not a new phenomena. However, it assumed importance because of various factors like rapid increase in the population, break-down of the joint family system, slow rate of construction and a large number of old houses which need replacement. The estimated housing demand (1901-71) and a summary of housing shortage 1951-71 in India are given in Tables 5 and 6.

Practically for many centuries the foreign government neglected the issues. The British have not shown any interest except providing accommodation to some of their staff in towns and cities. It was only after independence that government took interest in this respect. With the creation of a separate ministry at the centre, organised efforts were made. A statement on housing policy was made for the first time in the Parliament on 14th August, 1957.[3]

Public policy on housing in India is indicated in the five year plans. The plan document clarified that the State cannot afford to confine its role in the field of planning and regulation. Private enterprise is not in a position to do the jobs so far as low income groups are concerned. A large section of the country's population cannot afford to pay the rent for accommodation of even the minimum standards. The state has, therefore, to fill the gap and assist in the construction of suitable houses for low and middle income groups both in urban and rural areas as part of its own function. Accordingly, the government started two housing programmes as follows :

1. Public Sector Housing
2. Social Housing Schemes.

---

3. Government of India, 1975. *Housing the People*, Publication Division, New Delhi, p. 5.

TABLE 5

Estimated Housing Demand (1901 to 1971)

(in millions)

Year	*Total Demand*	*Indices*	*Rural Demand*	*Indices*	*Urban Demand*	*Indices*
1901	48 (100.0)	100	42 (87.5)	100	6 (12.5)	100
1911	50 (100.0)		45 (90.0)		5 (10.0)	
1921	50 (100.0)	104	45 (90.0)	107	5 (10.0)	83
1931	56 (100.0)	117	49 (87.5)	117	7 (12.5)	117
1941	64 (100.0)	133	55 (85.9)	131	9 (14.1)	150
1951	72 (100.0)	150	60 (83.3)	143	12 (16.7)	200
1961	88 (100.0)	183	72 (81.8)	171	16 (18.2)	267
1971	110 (100.0)	229	88 (80.0)	210	22 (20.0)	367

Note : Housing demand computed as : one housing unit for every five persons.

Source: Sinha, B. D. (1976), p. 115.

TABLE 6

Summary of Estimated Housing Shortage (1951 to 1971)

(in millions)

Items	*1951*	*1956*	*1961*	*1966*	*1977*
A. Demand (one unit per five persons)	72.220	79.720	87.840	98.220	109.580
B. Existing stock (inclusive of age-old structure)	64.362	70.128	79.223	85.179	92.458
C. Replacement requirement due to age	2.307	3.363	4.676	5.813	7.268
D. Available stock (exclusive of age-old structure) (B–C)	62.055	66.765	74.547	79.366	85.190
E. Housing Shortage (A–D)	10.165	12.955	13.293	18.854	24.390

Source : Sinha, B.D. (1976), p. 115.

Under Public Sector Housing, as the very name indicates, the activities and opportunities are restricted to the employees of the government and public organisations.

Social Housing Schemes cater to the needs of the people coming under the low and middle income groups and those belonging to economically weaker sections of society, both in rural and urban areas. The government has introduced nine Social Housing Schemes since 1952; they are :

(1) Integrated Subsidised Housing Scheme for Industrial Workers and Economically Weaker Sections of the Community (1952).
(2) Low Income Group Housing Scheme (1954).
(3) Subsidised Housing Scheme for Plantation Workers (1956) and (1967).
(4) Slum Clearance and Improvement Scheme (1956).
(5) Village Housing Project Scheme (1957).
(6) Middle Income Group Housing Scheme (1957).
(7) Rental Housing Scheme for State Government Employees (1959).
(8) Land Acquisition and Development Scheme (1959).
(9) Schemes for Provision of House Sites to Landless Workers in Rural Areas (1971).

Except the subsidised housing scheme for plantation workers, all other housing schemes are in the state sector. The Central Government provides financial assistance to states by way of 'block loans' and 'block grants'. However, in respect of the subsidised housing scheme for plantation workers, the Central Government provides financial assistance to the states directly but outside the plan allocations.

In addition to the schemes included for rural areas under Social Housing Schemes, as part of ameliorative measures for the socially weaker sections of society, the government has undertaken subsidised housing for SCs, STs and other Backward Classes and Handloom Workers. Some state governments have also launched special schemes involving mass participation to construct houses for the rural poor by granting them free house sites. Kerala's "one lakh housing scheme", the Andhra Pradesh's "co-operative housing scheme" for the SCs and STs, the Karnataka Government's "people's housing schemes" are schemes which have initiated new awareness among the rural people.

In the case of Mine Workers, housing programmes are being implemented with the help of labour welfare funds. The central departments like the Defence, Railways, Iron and Steel, Communication and Housing have all taken up housing programmes for their employees.

Details of various schemes for the urban dwellers are not included here but can be had from various studies conducted on urban population in different parts of the country.

The housing schemes that catter to the needs of rural people are :

(1) Village Housing Projects Scheme (1957).
(2) Subsidised Housing Scheme for Plantation Workers (1956 and 1967).
(3) Free House-sites for Landless Workers (1971).

The village housing project scheme was introduced to improve the housing conditions of rural people by the Central Government during 1957. Through this scheme, as a first step, the landless agricultural workers are given house-sites either free of cost or at a nominal price. They were also given loans to construct houses and financial aid was forthcoming for laying of roads and drains to improve the environmental conditions in the villages.

The scheme utilises locally available building materials along with the principle of self-help through the Community Development Block in selected villages. Monetary assistance is given to the extent of 80 per cent of the cost of construction to a maximum of Rs. 4,000 per house. Technical advice and guidance without charge are extended to villagers through the Rural Housing Cells and also by Block Development authorities.

The Plantation Labour Act, 1951 enforces that every planter should provide rent-free housing to the resident workers. Since all planters are not in a position to extend this facility, a scheme (Plantation Labour Housing Scheme) was introduced in 1956. The same was revised in 1966 and called 'Subsidised Housing Scheme for Plantation Workers'. Under this scheme planters are given loan to the extent of 50 per cent of the cost of construction along with 37.5 per cent subsidy. It was also provided that preference for subsidy will be given to those planters whose financial conditions warrant such a help. Under this scheme planters in South India were given a maximum of Rs. 3,200 per house while North Indian planters got Rs. 4,000 per house. Central Government assistance upto 90 per cent (65 per cent loan and 25 per cent as subsidy) of the approved cost of the house was available to plantation workers through housing co-operatives. Those planters with small estates are permitted to have joint housing colonies.

A scheme for free house sites to landless workers was initiated during 1971. The Government of India will give financial assistance for providing such benefits to landless workers in rural areas. Normally, a maximum of 100 square yards are allowed to each family.

A sum of Rs. 469.91 crores was spent on various social housing schemes till the end of the fourth five year plan. The fifth five year plan had an outlay of Rs. 580.16 crores for housing in both Central and State Sectors.

As is true of all the developing nations housing is given a very low priority by our planners. Housing was allotted a percentage of investment during the various five year plans which has been as follows :

First Five Year Plan	18 per cent
Second Five Year Plan	12 per cent
Third Five Year Plan	6-7 per cent
Fourth Five Year Plan	4 per cent

The outlay on housing schemes in the fifth five year plan touches only the fringe of the housing with 1.6 per cent of the plan outlay. A major part of these plan allocations has been directed to the urban areas. The allocation of funds when compared to the requirement is very small. Besides this the little money allotted has not been utilised fully; the problem, therefore, is not only of adequate financial provisions but also of ensuring that these funds are actually spent on housing in rural India.[4]

4. Chandhoke, S.K. : 1977, "Housing Conditions in Rural India", *IIC Quarterly*, Vol. 4, p. 174.

One of the features of housing in the country is that the building activity has been in the hands of private sector. Compared to the demand for housing the private sector cannot meet the same. Further, the costs of construction have gone up so high that the low income groups cannot afford to rent even a small house. Laws relating to taxation and rent control have discouraged investment of private capital in low cost housing.

Besides building construction undertaken by private persons, the Central Government is giving financial assistance to much of the housing activities. The other funding agency is the Life Insurance Corporation. In all such cases the State Governments are implementing the scheme while the union government exercise overall control.

Though cooperatives have a significant role to play in the field of rural housing, only in some states it has shown some progress to provide accommodation for the middle and low income groups. On the whole, the role of cooperative in rural areas is negligible.

One happy trend is that the circumstances have been changing recently in India. More funds are being made available for the implementation of the village housing projects scheme. Grants are being given for reviewing the old programme for the construction of demonstration houses in different parts of the country.

Under the village housing project scheme, villagers can apply for loans not exceeding 50 per cent of the total cost of the house with a ceiling of Rs. 1,500. This has been raised from time to time and stands now at Rs. 5,000 for each house. The other 50 per cent is also made good either in cash, materials, labour or all the three forms of assistance combined. The villager is responsible for construction and the state, apart from providing loan, supervises the work and gives some technical assistance by means of plans and specifications.

Another interesting development is the implementation of distribution of house-sites to landless agricultural labourers. The Housing and Urban Development Corporation (HUDCO) has come forward to finance the construction of different types of houses for landless agricultural workers.

The Reserve Bank of India has directed Nationalised Banks and Scheduled Commercial Banks to extend monetary assistance for social housing schemes like the Rural Housing Scheme. Preference will be given to those schemes which are intended to benefit the economically weaker sections of the community. The interest charged for these schemes are at concessional rates, about 2 per cent lower than the current rate.

A break up of houses under various schemes is given below:

Sl. No.	*Schemes*	*Year Intro-duced*	*No. of Houses*	
			Sanctioned	*Built by March 1973*
1.	Integrated subsidised housing scheme for industrial workers and economically weaker sections	1952	2,43,583	1,81,966
2.	Low income group housing scheme	1954	3,06,266	1,71,777
3.	Subsidised housing scheme for plantation workers	1956	14,297	2,139
4.	Slum clearance and improvement scheme	1956	1,49,404	1,06,262
5.	Village housing project scheme	1957	96,299	51,815
6.	Middle income group housing scheme	1959	44,036	28,366
7.	Rental housing scheme for state government employees	1959	28,776	20,500
8.	Jhuggi and Jhoumpri removal scheme—Delhi only	1960	N.A.	56,945*
9.	Free house-sites for landless workers	1971	N.A.	6,52,828*

N.A.=Not Available. *Not included in the total.

Against 8,82,661 houses sanctioned 5,62,825 houses have been completed, by March 1973.

Considering the difficulties encountered in implementing various schemes, which are related to the economic backwardness of the people who have no savings and the available scarce resources, the Fifth Five Year Plan restricted its role to the following limited objectives in the field of housing.

1. Preservation and improvement of the existing housing stock.
2. Continuance of the existing schemes to provide subsidised houses to certain weaker sections of the community.
3. Extension of support to institutional agencies such as HUDCO and Housing Boards to enable them to provide assistance to schemes for the benefit of low income and middle income groups.
4. Intensification of research and development of cheap building materials.
5. Provision of house-sites to four million landless labourers as part of minimum needs programme.

Along with the problem of money, the rural housing scheme is faced with the limited number of people with experience and orientation in matters of rural housing. Many seminars, symposia and conferences are being arranged to discuss the problems of rural housing and village planning in different regions of the country.

The Ford Foundation came forward to meet the initial demand of technical knowledge. A decision was taken to start special wings in some colleges and universities in the country to impart training, research and demonstration in rural housing. It was planned that technological and socio-ecological sciences were to be included in the scope of such schemes.

A central advisory committee was assigned with the task of co-ordinating the matters of training, research and extension. The work of this committee is supplemented with regional advisory boards which have the same significance.

There are at present four public sector organisations in the country, dealing with various aspects of housing, working under the Ministry of Works and Housing. They are :

1. National Buildings Organisations (NBO).
2. National Buildings Construction Corporation Limited (NBCC).
3. Housing and Urban Development Corporation Ltd. (HUDCO).
4. Hindustan Housing Factory (HHF).

The National Building Organisation set up in 1954 is co-ordinating and promoting the building research and its application. This organisation works in collaboration with the Planning Commission, Research Laboratories, Construction Departments and Housing Boards established by various State Governments. This organisation also acts as a UN Regional Housing Centre for the hot and arid zone of the Economic and Social Commission for Asia and the Pacific Region. Under this organisation (NBO) five rural housing wings at Howrah, Chandigarh, Anand, Bangalore and Delhi are working to provide technical assistance to the State Governments in rural housing and village planning programmes. These wings help evolve designs of low cost rural houses and such other types of buildings.

The National Building Construction Corporation (NBCC), though a private limited company which came into being in 1960, is now fully owned by the Government of India. According to one estimate, the Corporation had during 1973-74 jobs, worth Rs. 22.8 crores. But it could complete only jobs amounting to Rs. 8.4 crores leaving a huge unspent balance of Rs. 14.4 crores. Nevertheless, the turnover in 1973-74 (8.4 crores) represents three-fold increase in the average yearly turnover into 1970-71 and an increase of 40 per cent over the previous year's figures of Rs. 6.0 crores. Further the Corporation had plans to increase its activities to Rs. 20 crores by 1978-79.

The Housing and Urban Development Corporation Ltd. (HUDCO), a Government of India enterprise, was established in

1970. Some of its functions include for collecting and disseminating information and ideas on improved designs, construction methods and other innovations by having contact with research institutions like the Central Building Research Institute (CBRI) and the Structural Engineering Research Centre (SERC). The Corporation had sanctioned 181 schemes in 18 states and union territories by 1975 with a loan commitment of about Rs. 127.5 crores. The focus of the scheme was to help economically weaker sections and people who have low income of Rs. 600 or less. HUDCO has now extended its scheme to different areas of housing and its role is becoming complex.[5]

The Hindustan Housing Factory (HHF), another Central Government organisation, concentrates on the benefit of people for bringing down the cost and increasing the speed of construction.

The HHF has two very important achievements by producing (i) pre-fabricated industrial structures for Urban areas and (ii) pre-fabricated low cost structures for Rural areas.

5. Government of India, 1975, *Housing the People*, Publication Division, New Delhi.

3

Housing in Karnataka

DISCUSSIONS on rural housing generally includes house types and village settlement pattern. Broadly the natural regions of Karnataka are identified as follows:

(a) Coastal region	:	North and South Kanara Districts
(b) Malnad	:	Shimoga, Hassan, Chikmagalur and Coorg Districts
(c) Semi-Malnad	:	Some areas of Hassan, Mysore, Dharwar and Belgaum Districts
(d) Southern Maidan	:	Mandya, Bangalore, Chitradurga, Kolar, Tumkur and some parts of Mysore Districts
(e) Northern Maidan	:	Bijapur, Bidar, Gulbarga, Raichur and Bellary Districts

The State has been divided by Learmouth into four main economic regions viz , Coastal, Malnad, Southern Maidan and Northern Maidan.[1] He has further divided each region into a number of sub-regions based on certain characteristics like physical features, rainfall, kind of crops grown and so forth. However,

1. Census of India, 1961, Vol. I, Part IV-A (iii), Report on house types on village settlement pattern in India.

the layouts of villages and house types in the State discussed here refers to the five natural regions and all types of villages and houses normally found in different parts of the state.

The following are different forms of villages in the State.

(i) Villages with isolated homestead;

(ii) Villages with linear clusters;

(iii) Villages having several streets or lanes with linear arrangements of houses giving roughly a rectangular shape or a square shape to the village;

(iv) Villages of types (ii) together with shapeless clusters situated in one or more portions of the village.

The first type, *i.e.*, villages with isolated homesteads are found in the two coastal districts. The terrain in these districts is generally uneven. The houses are normally situated in or near the agricultural fields. The distance between houses vary from a few hundred yards to a furlong or more depending on the extent of land owned by individual cultivators.

Similar situation obtains in malnad regions. One of the special features in these areas is that a small bazar will be found for each village or a group of 2-3 small villages. People come to such places for purchasing their necessities or for recreational purposes. Schools and places of worship will be located at important centres of the villages. The households are identified by different family names or other names of descriptive nature. Footpaths are very many. However, in some places a few house clusters are also found.

In other regions of the state, the most common type is that villages with many streets in which the houses are built on either sides. Here, the number of streets depend on the number of castes and the population of the village. The streets generally have the name of the predominant caste in the street. The residential area of the village fixed up at the time of the first settlement by and large remains the same. Very often the houses and streets are congested. Only rich farmers are having backyards. The streets in many villages are as old as the settlement itself. Recently the village panchayats are regulating construction of houses and roads.

A normal feature observed in all the regions is that the scheduled castes generally live exclusively in groups. Often their houses are located either in a corner of the village or even a little away from the village and seldom close to caste Hindu locality. They also have separate drinking water wells. Till recently the government policy was to construct separate wells and in some places open separate schools exclusively for these communities.

With regard to location of temples, they ought to face either east or north and normally located in the centre of the village or where the clean or higher castes live. Similarly village schools, recreational centres and community halls are located in the central places.

In the *maidan* region, such as Mysore, Bangalore, Mandya, Kolar and Tumkur Districts, there are a number of irrigation tanks at the outskirts of the village. Villagers utilise tank water for domestic purposes.

One common feature is that villages are usually located on the banks of river, streams or near ponds. As already described most of the villages in the State have a number of streets depending on the population. The village has an irregular geometrical shape in its outer boundaries though sometimes the village has a ractangle or square form.

The houses in rural areas of the State can broadly be classified into two types on the basis of the nature of the ground plan and roof. They are building with :

(i) Rectangular ground plan with flat roof, and
(ii) Rectangular ground plan with sloping roof.

Buildings under type (i) are in large number in the Districts of :

1. Kolar	4. Bijapur	7. Bidar
2. Chitradurga	5. Gulbarga	8. Bellary
3. Dharwar	6. Raichur	9. Tumkur

Where the average annual rainfall is about 625 mms or less. The material used for the roof varies according to the economic conditions of the persons living in the houses. People with small income construct the roof using materials like tufts, reeds, bamboo, matting and odd courses of leaves to prevent the earth from dropping. A layer of earth is spread over and often it is plastered. One or two earthenware pots without bottom made by the local potter are kept side by side in a line in the roof to facilitate the smoke to go out. Apart from this the roof has a number of small square openings. This is provided for ventilation and during rainy days they are covered with broken earthen pots. Those who can afford to have stone slabs together use lime mortar or cement for roof. However, more than 75 per cent of the houses have flat roof with mud or materials like reeds in these districts. In the districts of Kolar, Gulbarga and some parts of Bangalore roofs have slab because stone slabs are easily available in these regions.

In the Districts of Mysore, Mandya, Hassan, Coorg, South Kanara, Chikmagalur, Shimoga, Belgaum, North Kanara and parts of Bangalore the type (ii) buildings having rectangular ground plan with sloping roof are more predominant. The reason is that in these districts the rain fall is moderate to heavy. Heavy rainfall ranging from 3000-6250 mms is recorded in the coastal districts and Malnad regions of the State. In these districts the houses are provided with steep roofs.

Where rainfall is relatively less *i.e.*, in Mysore, Mandya and Bangalore districts, there is a type of inclined roof made up of four slopes. These houses are locally called *Thottimane* with *Verandah* in the front where people sit, squat and sleep. Inside the house there is sufficient ventilation, as a quadrangular open place in middle of the house is formed where all the four slopes project downwards. These houses are very accommodative and meet the requirements of farmers. Though there are not many rooms, the agricultural implements and cattle can be kept inside the house. The roofs are covered with semi-cylindrical country tiles made by local potter. Another type of house locally called *kavalige mane* has two inclined planes. Country titles or Mangalore tiles are used for roofs depending upon the economic conditions of the owner. The name Mangalore tile has nothing to do with Mangalore town with regard to the manufacturing of the tiles. There are factories in other parts of the state where such pressed tiles are produced.

The houses having inclined roofs by and large have roofs thatched with one or the other innumerable varieties of grass locally available. Many a time dried leaves of coconut palms, arecanut palms, date palms and dried sugar cane leaves are used. Details of predominant material of roof in Rural and Urban areas are given in Table 7.

The materials used for the walls of the houses depend upon two main factors :

(i) availability of the materials used, and
(ii) economic conditions of the owner or resident.

Taking the first factor into consideration it is found that mud walls are more predominant in the rural areas in the districts of :

1. Bangalore
2. Chikmagalur
3. Coorg
4. Dharwar
5. Hassan
6. Kolar
7. Mandya
8. Mysore
9. North Kanara
10. Shimoga
11. South Kanara
12. Tamkur

In the district of Belgaum, Bellary, Bidar, Bijapur, Chitradurga, Gulbarga and Raichur the stone walls are more predominant. Even rich people construct walls with rough stones which are available cheaply in these areas. In the districts where mud walls are constructed, the construction process shows small difference. In some districts mud lumps are used for wall construction. These lumps approximately 1-1½ feet height are put over one another and allowed to dry up after each course. In some areas, a frame is constructed first with split bamboo and mud filled into the interslices. These types are thin but are strong. Details of

TABLE 7

Predominant Material of Roof

(*Every 1000 Houses*)

State/District	*Rural*			*Urban*		
	a	*b*	*c*	*a*	*b*	*c*
KARNATAKA	553	446	1	245	753	2
1. Bangalore	331	669	—	84	916	—
2. Belgaum	390	609	1	154	846	—
3. Bellary	900	99	1	738	260	2
4. Bidar	531	459	10	331	638	31
5. Bijapur	958	42	—	761	236	3
6. Chikmagalur	342	658	—	74	926	—
7. Chitradurga	617	382	1	213	786	1
8. Coorg	351	649	—	78	921	1
9. Dharwar	710	289	1	385	611	4
10. Gulbarga	679	316	5	295	686	19
11. Hassan	172	828	—	54	945	1
12. Kolar	492	508	—	197	801	2
13. Mandya	245	754	1	226	774	—
14. Mysore	240	760	—	61	939	—
15. North Kanara	571	429	—	151	849	—
16. Raichur	942	55	3	764	236	—
17. Shimoga	500	499	1	100	900	—
18. South Kanara	596	404	—	121	879	—
19. Tumkur	658	342	—	173	827	—

Note : a—Gross, leaves, reeds, bamboo, thatch, mud, unburnt bricks, wood.
b—Tiles, slate, shingle, corrugated sheets, asbestos sheets, concrete
c—Others

Source: Census of India 197I Series 14, Mysore, Part IV, Report on Housing.

TABLE 8

Number of Houses per 1000 Census Houses in the Districts by Major Wall Material

State/District	*Grass, leaves, reeds and bamboo*	*Mud*	*Unburnt Bricks*	*Burnt Bricks*	*Stone*
KARNATAKA	68	334	71	160	357
1. Bangalore	5	247	158	553	35
2. Belgaum	43	137	102	65	636
3. Bellary	157	95	24	40	677
4. Bidar	29	111	—	1	849
5. Bijapur	35	40	3	4	912
6. Chikmagalur	145	554	22	239	30
7. Chitradurga	141	144	118	160	427
8. Coorg	95	514	36	330	15
9. Dharwar	87	306	173	76	350
10. Gulbarga	28	40	1	18	900
11. Hassan	39	804	3	123	27
12. Kolar	21	240	217	245	257
13. Mandya	11	624	5	185	169
14. Mysore	49	712	2	224	10
15. North Kanara	227	528	14	35	161
16. Raichur	106	191	29	27	640
17. Shimoga	251	428	25	210	76
18. South Kanara	37	747	24	14	173
19. Tumkur	43	360	114	194	285

Source : Census of India 1971, Series 14; Mysore, Part IV, Report on Housing.

major wall material in different districts are given in Table.

From the above, it is seen that in the regions with heavy rainfall especially malnad and the coastal belt, houses will have steep inclined roofs. In the northern maidan region houses with flat roofs are predominant. In the southern maidan region the roofs are sloped since the average annual rainfall is not more than 750 mms. In the *semi-malnad* region the houses have the characteristics of both malnad and maidan region.

Housing and the economic condition of the residents have relevance. It is better to describe at different levels how money is utilised for the housing needs. The materials that are used to construct the house need the money in all respects. In other words, the physical structure of a house is very much rather purely related with the economic condition of the rural population.

The poor and the houseless have small huts built up of non-durable materials as well as easily perishable material, mostly mud and thatchs. A typical rural house has mud walls and floor which are made by hand. Neither sufficient foundation nor adequate projections are provided and gradually destroyed by rains, winds and floods. These walls have a thatched roof which generally consists of a defective bearing frame of jungle wood or bamboo covered by layers of thatch.

Another common roof variety is the flat mud roof—a flat structure of poles and reeds bearing a thick layer of mud. The life of the roof is very short as the wood frames are too weak for the load they support. As a whole people live in place where human beings cannot live or which is unsuitable for the life of human beings. These houses are identified as *kachcha* houses.[2] It is here of much importance to explain the meanings and differentiation between *kachcha* and *pucca* occurs among houses only on the basis of the kind of material that are used to construct the house. The major distinction between the two is that the *kachcha* houses are built with non-durable materials. Whereas the *pucca*

2. Rene F. Fyhralde : "Rural Housing in India" in T. J. Manickam *Urban and Rural Planning Thought*, Vol. III, No. 4, 1960, pp. 150-153.

houses are built with durable materials, having life expectancy.

Chandhoke[3] has distinguished the materials that can be called as *kachcha* and those as *pucca*. The non-durable materials (*kachcha* houses) are grass leaves, reeds or bamboo, thatchwood, mud, unburnt bricks and so forth. The houses constructed out of these materials need constant repairs and their roofs especially are highly prone to fire hazards entertaining considerable amount of strain on the villager both financially and otherwise. The size of this house is small always. They have either single room or two rooms like accommodation. Since non-durable materials are used both for the wall and roofs, and as they are in a position of being destroyed easily, they would be threatening the life of those who live under such roofs. People under those roofs lack not only economic security but also physical security.

Pucca houses are those houses built with durable and long lasting materials such as stones, burnt bricks and lime, cement concrete, asbestos cement sheets, corrugated iron, zinc or other metal sheets. These are relatively bigger in size, some are having upstairs terrace and more than three rooms. They have other facilities such as space, water and drainage facilities, bathrooms, lavatories. Normally repairs are needed after a long period of construction. People living in these houses have security for their properties as well as their lives as both the walls and roof are enduring.

House construction with *pucca* materials are found less frequently in villages. They are owned by a few rural rich people namely the agriculturists. It can be safely concluded that *pucca* houses are of rich people houses and *kachcha* houses are generally of poor people.

Semi structure is seen as things do not stick always to pure forms. Thus, other than purely *kachcha* and purely *pucca* houses are also found in the rural areas. These are owned by middle

---

3. Chandhoke, S.K. : "Housing Conditions in Rural India", *ICC Quarterly*, Vol. 4, No. 2, 1977, p. 172.

income groups or people whose income are just above the poverty line. The semi-durable nature of the materials used to build such houses carry such names. These materials are neither perishable nor long lasting. For example, country made tile is a material often used to build houses which are partly durable and partly non-durable in character. These semi type houses have more than one room and the walls may be built with burnt bricks but the roofs with *kachcha* materials. Sometimes, there are houses where the main hall or room is constructed with concrete or burnt bricks or title and the other rooms of thatches. Particulars of number of rooms and persons per room are given in Table 9.

TABLE 9

The Proportion of Households Living in one room, or in 2 to 5 rooms and the persons per room in the Rural and Urban Areas of the State

Households living in houses with	*Proportion of such households to total No. of households in the State*		*No. of persons per room*	
	Rural	*Urban*	*Rural*	*Urban*
	%	%		
1 room	51.4	41.3	4.99	4.72
2 rooms	31.8	30.8	3.00	2.91
3 rooms	10.3	13.8	2.41	2.21
4 rooms	3.8	7.1	2.03	1.78
5 rooms	2.7	7.0	1.47	1.25

Source : Census of India 1971, Series 14, Mysore, Part IV, Report on Housing.

Brick walls with tiled roofs are also seen. These houses may not be long lasting like *pucca* houses, and not be easily destroyed like *kachcha* houses. The semi-*pucca* or semi-*kachcha* houses are numbering more than pure *pucca* houses but less than pure *kachcha* houses.

While distinctions are possible between *kachcha* and *pucca* houses it is impossible between the *kachcha* house and the houseless people. A slight variation in the literal meaning for houseless is necessary to some extent in the present context. We cannot be carried away by the meaning as houseless have no house at all. Details of tenure status in rural and urban areas are given in Table 10. Of course, the houseless are with homes but still live in

TABLE 10

Distribution of 1000 Census Households Living in Census According to Tenure Status in Rural Areas

State/District	*Tenure Status*			
	Rural		*Urban*	
	Owned	*Rented*	*Owned*	*Rented*
KARNATAKA	867	133	447	553
1. Bangalore	872	128	294	706
2. Belgaum	906	94	542	458
3. Bellary	888	112	603	397
4. Bidar	965	35	724	276
5. Bijapur	891	109	560	440
6. Chikmagalur	722	278	467	533
7. Chitradurga	932	68	483	517
8. Coorg	581	419	307	693
9. Dharwar	884	116	509	491
10. Gulbarga	918	82	526	474
11. Hassan	911	89	474	526
12. Kolar	936	64	379	621
13. Mandya	911	89	555	445
14. Mysore	934	66	460	540
15. North Kanara	883	117	539	461
16. Raichur	898	102	643	357
17. Shimoga	874	126	361	639
18. South Kanara	435	565	395	605
19. Tumkur	928	72	499	501

Source : Census of India, 1971, Series 14, Mysore, Part IV, Report on Housing.

other land or places in very small huts which are built with *kachcha* material. For clear distinction houseless people would be taken into account under the category of *kachcha* houses. In the same way, there is less difference between people who live in *pucca* houses and those who live in *Janata* houses. *Janata* houses built under the government house programme has been always *pucca* houses as the *pucca* materials are utilised.

These are the things seen in reality therefore, the problem of housing should be viewed from two angles namely houseless and people in *kachcha* houses. The simple provision of house sites or some construction materials to economically poor people or the economically weaker sections of the population above will not solve the problem on any account. Attention should be focussed on reconstructing the existing bad conditioned *kachcha* houses and there is a need to give equal weightage to these two groups.

4

Rural Houseless—Background

THIS CHAPTER focuses attention on the background of rural houseless in Karnataka. To begin with details of villages, population in rural areas, number of houseless families and the houses built for the benefit of poor in each district of the state have been given. The problem of housing and its necessity as assessed by the villagers have been discussed. If they are not having a house how long they are without a house, where do they live and the social standing of such people are included here. Knowledge of government schemes for houseless, number of those who were benefitted, year of availing of such benefit, dimension and cost of the site or house have further been discussed. Their opinion about the scheme, procedure of allotment and the role of government and panchayats in this regard are also included in this chapter.

The state had a houseless population of 1,16,701 in 1971. Among them 87,775 villages. A large number of these houseless people. Details of houseless population in different districts of the state are given in Table 11.

It could be seen from the table that a considerable number of families are facing this problem in all the 19 districts of the state. While some progress has been made in some districts by way of providing them with free sites and help them to construct their houses under various housing schemes explained in the previous chapter, the number of houseless is increasing year after year.

HOUSELESS POPULATION

In the State there are 38,274 houseless households comprising of 116,701 persons. The houseless population in the district are indicated in statement below :

TABLE 11

Houseless Households and Population in the Districts

State/District	*Total Rural Urban*	*Houseless Population*	
		No. of Households	*Persons*
KARNATAKA	Total	31,274	1,16,701
	Rural	25,101	87,775
	Urban	13,173	27,926
1. Bangalore	Total	5,872	11,270
	Rural	1,117	3,213
	Urban	4,745	8,057
2. Belgaum	Total	2,252	7,987
	Rural	1,605	6,118
	Urban	647	1,869
3. Bellary	Total	1,421	3,120
	Rural	662	1,909
	Urban	759	1,211
4. Bidar	Total	1,248	4,557
	Rural	1,171	4,291
	Urban	77	266
5. Bijapur	Total	2,301	8,934
	Rural	1,789	7,734
	Urban	512	1,197
6. Chikmagalur	Total	887	2,447
	Rural	641	1,734
	Urban	368	1,125

State/District	Total Rural Urban	Houseless Population No. of Households	Persons
7. Chitradurga	Total	1,363	4,423
	Rural	995	3,298
	Urban	368	1,125
8. Coorg	Total	445	995
	Rural	264	571
	Urban	181	424
9. Dharwar	Total	4,011	14,029
	Rural	2,746	10,376
	Urban	1,265	3,653
10. Gulbarga	Total	4,057	14,712
	Rural	3,796	14,086
	Urban	261	696
11. Hassan	Total	1,057	3,120
	Rural	116	2,534
	Urban	241	586
12. Kolar	Total	2,045	5,083
	Rural	1,380	3,575
	Urban	665	1,508
13. Mandya	Total	1,411	4,048
	Rural	953	3,008
	Urban	458	1,040
14. Mysore	Total	1,642	4,566
	Rural	942	2,793
	Urban	707	1,773
15. North Kanara	Total	1,254	5,040
	Rural	987	4,228
	Urban	277	812

(*Continued*)

State/District	*Total Rural Urban*	*Houseless Population*	
		No. of Households	*Persons*
16. Raichur	Total	2,890	10,132
	Rural	2,580	9,189
	Urban	310	943
17. Shimoga	Total	1,527	6,116
	Rural	1,141	1,141
	Urban	386	1,216
18. South Kanara	Total	1,449	2,821
	Rural	674	1,713
	Urban	775	1,108
19. Tumkur	Total	1,125	3,231
	Rural	832	2,501
	Urban	293	730

Source : Census of India 1971, Series 14, Mysore Part II A, General Population Tables.

This may be attributed to the growing population in rural areas and the continued impoverishment of villagers. In the recent past—1980 onwards—not much emphasis is laid on the governmental housing scheme for the benefit of rural poor. If the same trend continues the number of houseless is bound to shoot up abnormally. The problem is caught in vicious circle and unless it is tackled on war footing it will be hard task for any government to combat the situation in the near future.

The problem of housing is closely linked with the land holding pattern in villages. Land is prestigious commodity in rural situation. Ownership of landed property determines the social and economic status of families. In the same way those who have no place to live under are looked down. Therefore, the life ambition of every individual in the village is to acquire a piece of land or to own atleast a place to live. Nevertheless, the presence of such large number of houseless population poses a challenge in any society.

In every village some are without houses. Out of one hundred villages included in the study, all have houseless families. Nearly 80.4 per cent respondents have confirmed this fact and housing problems in the village.

In view of the above the study included 1516 (51.8 per cent) houseless along with 1264 (43.2 per cent) who have been given *Janata* house. Districtwise sample houses are given in Table 12.

TABLE 12

Ownership Pattern

Sl. No.	*Name of the District*	*Kachcha house*	*Pucca house*	*Janata house*	*House-less*	*Total*
1.	Bangalore	1	—	169	180	350
2.	Chikmagalur	2	1	152	73	228
3.	Chitradurga	2	3	137	119	261
4.	Coorg	2	1	84	34	121
5.	Hassan	4	6	110	112	232
6.	Kolar	9	11	134	195	349
7.	Mandya	14	13	88	126	241
8.	Mysore	4	3	70	227	304
9.	Shimoga	10	7	123	160	300
10.	South Kanara	10	7	110	114	241
11.	Tumkur	23	11	87	176	297
	Total	81 (2.7)	63 (2.1)	1264 (43.2)	1516 (51.8)	2924

The necessity to own a dwelling house has been indicated by a large majority of the people. This has already been explained early. Villagers consider that it is one of the basic necessities. When asked to explain whether they feel insecure because they are without a house, all the houseless respondents have expressed in the affirmative. This reaction is but natural because the houseless are under the obligation of people who have given them shelter, Moreover, their social status will be low if they are not owning a house and therefore this need will create a gap.

What is heartening is that majority of the houseless are, by tradition living without any house. This has been sustained by the findings of the survey. A look at the data, showing the caste composition of the respondents reveals that about 45.4 per cent houseless composed of scheduled caste groups. Another 55.2 per cent of *Janata* house residents have given their caste names as SC. Therefore it is clear that the people from downtrodden communities are the worst effected in rural areas of the State. Details are given in Table 13.

TABLE 13

Caste Composition of Respondents

Sl. No.	*Caste*	*Janata*	*Houseless*	*Others*	*Total*
1.	Panikar/Nair	1	4	—	5
2.	Coorg	—	—	1	1
3.	Gudigara	1	—	1	2
4.	Maggadavaru/Nekara/ Devanga	8	9	1	18
5.	Ganiga	3	4	1	8
6.	Ura/Arasu	3	5	3	11
7.	Beda	1	2	—	3
8.	Budubudike	—	2	—	2
9.	Balegara Jogi	6	7	—	13
10.	Scheduled Tribe	5	3	—	8
11.	Harijan/Bhovi/Korama/ Koracha	698	689	21	1408
12.	Halumatha/Kuruba	30	32	6	68
13.	Maratha	8	11	1	20
14.	Vokkaliga/Kunchitaga/ Reddi	52	68	37	157
15.	Bant/Shetty	11	5	3	19
16.	Lingayat/Banajiga/Reddy	38	40	16	94

Sl. No.	*Caste*	*Janata*	*Houseless*	*Others*	*Total*
17.	Brahmin	10	39	7	56
18.	Vishwakarma	19	37	1	57
19.	Madivala/Dhobi	25	25	1	51
20.	Bestha/Gangematha/ Mogaveera	29	14	2	45
21.	Padmasale/Bhajantri/ Barber	12	17	—	29
22.	Golla	1	19	3	23
23.	Tigala/Togataveera	9	25	2	36
24.	Bhillava	11	5	—	16
25.	Ediga	13	19	4	36
26.	Uppara	18	16	1	35
27.	Vysya/Shetty	5	8	3	16
28.	Naika	55	90	1	146
29.	Kumbara	14	30	—	44
30.	Naidu	1	5	—	6
31.	Modaliyar	1	—	—	1
32.	Rajput	1	—	—	1
33.	Bhandari	1	—	—	1
34.	Dasaru	1	—	—	1
35.	Samagara	1	—	—	1
36.	Devadiga	1	5	—	6
37.	Kadu Konkani	—	1	—	1
38.	Boya	7	4	—	11
39.	Baniya	—	1	—	1
40.	Konkanigowda	2	1	—	3
41.	Kola	—	1	—	1
42.	Koliga	—	1	—	1
43.	Balachda	—	1	—	1
44.	Muslim	113	103	7	223
45.	Christian	12	7	1	20
46.	Others	6	9	—	15
47.	No Response	31	152	20	203
	Total	1264 (43.2)	1516 (51.8)	144 (4.9)	2924

The houseless by and large not only suffer from the stigma attached to their low caste status but have given other reasons for their inferior status, See Table 14. About 34.2 per cent houseless have indicated that their poor economic conditions pushed them to low social status. Some 19.3 per cent say that their dependance on others for such basic things as housing reduced their social standing. Another 14.5 per cent consider that they are under obligation and hence inferor in the village. For about 12.8 per cent houseless respondents their position is weak because they are immigrants in the place of their present residence. Usually the residential pattern of the village community consists of kin groups extended as caste groups. Normally, villagers would not like to leave their ancestral house, since that would bring some criticism. Those who go out of village often move to city. But if they are going to another village they are looked down. In the case of 18.8 per cent houseless respondents, all the above aspects are given as reasons.

The pattern of houselessness indicates that they are not having a house of their own for a number of years. In some cases their family had no place to live for generations. The study has 78.4 per cent households who have indicated that they are remaining without a house for the past 8 or more years. Details, regarding the period of remaining without a house are given in Table 15. The districts of Bangalore and Chitradurga have above 90 per cent respondents without owning a house for more than 8 years. Hassan, Mysore and South Kanara districts have about 80 per cent in this category. Even the remaining districts with the exception of Chikmagalur have relatively very high percentage. On an average about 70 per cent families are houseless for more than 8 years.

If the respondents are houseless, it is relevant to ask where do they live at present. While 32.4 per cent are living with their relatives, about 26.3 per cent have been given shelter by their friends. Strong kinship ties exist in rural parts and hence at times of distress, usually relatives come to the rescue. The normal pattern of friendship is that they belong to the same caste groups. Hence

TABLE 14

Houseless People are Looked Down Because of

Sl. No.	Name of the District	Poverty	Dependency	Obligation	Outsider	All	No Response	Total
1.	Bangalore	80	16	26	6	50	2	180
2.	Chikmagalur	24	19	4	7	19	—	73
3.	Chitradurga	52	30	12	14	11	—	119
4.	Coorg	6	7	1	19	1	—	34
5.	Hassan	63	8	20	13	8	—	112
6.	Kolar	75	32	19	29	40	—	195
7.	Mandya	22	21	28	22	33	—	126
8.	Mysore	63	62	30	17	55	—	227
9.	Shimoga	45	47	30	15	23	—	160
10.	South Kanara	39	24	20	25	6	—	114
11.	Tumkur	50	28	30	28	40	—	176
	Total	519	294	220	195	286	2	1516
	Percentage	34.2	19.3	14.5	12.8	18.8	0.1	

TABLE 15

Number of Years Without House

Sl. No.	Name of the District	One year	Two years	Three years	Four years	Five years	Six years	Seven years	Eight or more years	No response	Total
1.	Bangalore	3	2	3	1	3	2	1	162	3	180
2.	Chikmagalur	3	3	8	1	7	4	2	42	3	73
3.	Chitradurga	—	2	2	—	2	—	1	107	5	119
4.	Coorg	2	—	2	1	3	—	1	24	1	34
5.	Hassan	3	1	—	—	10	3	2	90	3	112
6	Kolar	1	9	2	6	13	11	3	141	9	195
7.	Mandya	4	4	11	4	4	6	3	88	2	126
8.	Mysore	3	4	3	3	5	5	19	180	5	227
9.	Shimoga	5	6	2	3	6	9	—	125	4	160
10.	South Kanara	3	1	1	2	5	1	1	93	7	114
11.	Tumkur	5	3	3	8	13	5	1	138	—	176
	Total	32	35	37	29	71	46	34	1190	42	1516
	Percentage	2.1	2.3	2.4	1.9	4.6	3.0	2.2	78.49	2.7	

large number of them live with their caste men. Village social structure and the residential pattern also support this trend. The 17 per cent under 'others' category mostly consist of patron-client situation.

A section of village population who are landless and houseless work under rich agriculturists. These farmers allow the landless to put up a 'hut' structure on their farm land. The beneficiaries are under constant obligation of landlords. Even though the land owners are benefitted, these days, due to fear of land reform laws, the 'clients' are being ejected. This trend is causing great incovenience and untold hardships to the poor houseless. Yet, there is another category—23.8 per cent who are not living with any one. These people are normally taking shelter in the deserted and delapidated structures in and around the village. They often cook their food under a tree or by using the side walls of old stone structures near temple and move over during nights to whatever shelter available. Details of present place of residence of the houseless population in the sample are shown in Table 16.

Poverty is the main reason for remaining houseless in the case of 75 per cent respondents. Those who have stated 'no site' account for 10.6 per cent. This group of houseless have some capacity to spend little money and labour to construct their own house, but they cannot afford to purchase land in the village. As discussed already, majority of houseless are SCs. Social discrimination is rampant in village India. The caste Hindus will not allow an untouchable or an SC to construct his house in the village. SCs have to squeeze within the traditional residential area. This is often demarcated either by a road or located away from the main village. Hence, they cannot dream of owning a site even when they are in a position to construct a house. About 12.8 per cent are immigrants and have expressed that they are not in a position to own a house in the village.

The fact that though migration took place 5-6 years back (59.1 per cent) they continue to live with their relatives, friends and others, explains the poor condition of immigrants in the village. Only 17.9 per cent have migrated one year back. Therefore, rural to rural migration is hampered in India. If migrants

TABLE 16

Presently Living With

Sl.No.	Name of the District		Relatives	Friends	Others	With no one	Total
1.	Bangalore	..	101	64	5	10	180
2.	Chikmagalur	..	12	35	8	18	73
3.	Chitradurga	..	30	12	24	53	119
4.	Coorg	..	4	6	18	6	34
5.	Hassan	..	32	43	28	9	112
6.	Kolar	..	82	53	25	35	195
7.	Mandya	..	40	29	23	34	126
8.	Mysore	..	60	49	33	85	227
9.	Shimoga	..	54	40	32	34	160
10.	South Kanara	..	24	25	42	23	114
11.	Tumkur	..	53	44	25	54	176
	Total	..	492	400	263	361	1516
	Percentage	..	32.4	26.3	17.3	23.8	

are not in a position to improve their economic and social condition in villages, naturally the rate of such migration will be less.

Both the central and the state governments have been implementing various schemes for the benefit of rural poor. The department of Social Welfare introduced programmes to weaker sections of population giving preference to SCs and STs. From 1971 onwards the central government has issued instructions to state governments to help the landless agricultural labourers to own at least a site and later encourage them to construct houses on these sites. During 1972 a scheme under "peoples' housing" was introduced. Details of these schemes are given in Chaper III.

The study envisaged to find out the popularity of these schemes in villages. Accordingly the people were asked whether they know the government assistance to poor in rural areas. Encouragingly about 80 per cent are aware of the schemes. Figures for different schemes are given in Table 17.

About 44 per cent are aware of facilities like free house site, *Janata* houses, monetary assistance for constructing one's own house, and assistance like construction materials from the government, panchayat and block development offices. Another 21.3 per cent are aware of free house-sites, *Janata* houses and construction material. While 4.6 per cent say, they are aware of distribution of free housesites only, about 4.0 per cent admitted, they know the scheme like free sites, houses and construction materials.

Villagers mostly came to know the schemes mentioned about through government officials. Only 8.5 per cent respondents have stated that the village panchayat gave them these details. About 30.9 per cent did not respond to this question. Perhaps periodical meetings arranged by revenue officials including the persons in charge of rural development programme in the village might have helped some villagers in getting details.

What is surprising is that only a small number have stated that they came to know these details from village panchayats. This needs further probing into the working of the local self government institutions.

While people are aware of schemes provided for their benefit,

TABLE 17

Knowledge of Government Assistance

Sl. No.	Name of the District	Free house sites	Houses	Monetary help	Construction material	HS/H/MH/&CM	HS/H & CM	HS/H MH	MH & C. Mat.	No response	Don't know	Total
1.	Bangalore	19	—	—	1	108	4	1	5	197	15	350
2.	Chikmagalur	2	—	—	1	173	1	30	—	19	2	228
3.	Chitradurga	7	—	—	1	112	1	—	3	137	—	261
4.	Coorg	—	—	—	1	110	—	—	—	7	3	121
5.	Hassan	2	1	—	—	160	1	—	—	56	12	232
6.	Kolar	1	1	2	—	9	308	—	—	28	—	349
7.	Mandya	—	—	—	93	147	—	—	—	1	—	241
8.	Mysore	69	—	—	2	166	7	—	2	57	1	304
9.	Shimoga	28	—	—	—	119	1	86	1	60	5	300
10.	South Kanara	9	10	—	—	186	4	—	1	31	—	241
11.	Tumkur	—	—	—	—	—	297	—	—	—	—	297
	Total	137	12	2	99	1290	624	117	12	593	38	2924
	Percentage	4.6	0.4	0.6	3.3	44.1	21.3	4.0	0.4	20.2	1.2	

HS=House site H=House MH=Monetary help CM=Construction material

Government also claims that nearly 14 lakh house sites are distributed and as as many 3 lakh *Janata* houses have been contructed till 1980. The study wanted to verify whether the really deserving are benefitted. Barring few a negligible number of families in the sample (1.1 per cent) are recipients of sites. The rest have not availed the benefit under free house site scheme. Those who got some construction material account for 2.5 per cent of the sample and other schemes like monetary assistance for constructing house, have not been mentioned by them at all.

The only significant aspect in the recent past is the introduction of the "Peoples' Housing Scheme". Despite the inherent drawbacks, some families have been benefitted. In this study about 43.5 per cent of the sample come under this category. Refer Table 18. These benefits have been drawn by the respondents in the last 6 years.

In the case of 35 families who got free sites from government, 27 are measuring 20′×30′. The average cost of each is estimated between Rs. 100-200. Only 8 families in the same got sites measuring 30′×40′ each. The estimated cost, of these larger dimension sites works out to Rs. 200-300 each. However, data regarding the dimension of the site and approximate cost of the site are based on the information supplied by the persons concerned and are subject to variation.

In the sample there are 1264 families who have been allotted *Janata* houses in the villages. While the dimension of the house varies from one region to another, the cost of the house has shown some normalcy. This is because of the government subsidy which was fixed while constructing different series. About 53.8 per cent houses are evaluated between Rs. 1501 to 2000 each. Nearly 20.1 per cent houses cost Rs. 2001 to 2500 each. There are 6.2 per cent houses in the range of Rs. 2501 to 3000. Houses, costing Rs. 1001 to 1500 each accounted 17.5 per cent.

As stated already most of the beneficiaries have recognised governmental help in this regard. They have mentioned that it is the government officials who have helped them in the allotment of the *Janata* houses. Only 2 per cent said panchayat came forward.

TABLE 18

Housing Benefits Availed

Sl. No.	Name of the Distrtct		Free Site	Janata House	Construction material	Not availed	Total
1.	Bangalore	..	1	169	—	180	350
2.	Chikmagalur	..	1	152	2	73	228
3.	Chitradurga	..	1	137	7	116	261
4.	Coorg	..	2	84	5	30	121
5.	Hassan	..	—	110	8	114	232
6.	Kolar	..	5	134	10	200	349
7.	Mandya	..	2	88	5	146	241
8.	Mysore	..	11	70	4	219	304
9.	Shimoga	..	3	123	15	159	300
10.	South Kanara	..	5	110	11	115	241
11.	Tumkur	..	4	97	9	187	297
	Total	..	35	1274	76	1539	2924
	Percentage	..	1.1	43.5	2.5	52.6	

Housing Benefits—Year Sanctioned

Sl. No.	*Name of the District*	*This year only*	*Last year*	*Two years back*	*Three years back*	*Four years back*	*Five years back*	*Six years back*	*Don't remember*	*No response*	*Not applicable*	*Total*
1.	Bangalore	1	2	3	81	17	107	5	3	1	180	350
2.	Chikmagalur	—	11	2	10	19	7	68	37	1	73	228
3.	Chitradurga	1	22	18	31	15	38	—	6	14	116	261
4.	Coorg	3	11	6	7	28	9	17	1	9	30	121
5.	Hassan	4	17	33	16	7	24	8	1	8	114	232
6.	Kolar	9	27	4	39	37	1	14	9	9	200	349
7.	Mandya	—	2	18	58	2	1	1	8	5	146	241
8.	Mysore	—	1	1	10	18	34	—	19	2	219	304
9.	Shimoga	—	11	10	9	20	19	43	19	10	159	300
10.	South Kanara	4	8	38	18	10	12	16	12	8	115	241
11.	Tumkur	2	26	8	17	8	10	22	13	4	187	297
	Total	24	138	141	246	181	262	194	128	71	1539	2924
	Percentage	0.8	4.7	4.8	8.4	6.1	8.9	6.6	4.3	2.4	52.6	

A large majority of the beneficiaries appreciated the role of officials who helped them secure concessions from government. In the days of widespread discontentment among people on the working of government, the present study and the opinion of people is revealing. Time and again, lot of criticism is being made about the corrupt practices and other shortcomings in the government departments. Nevertheless, the poor villagers expressed altogether different opinion.

Even the procedure of allotment of house is convenient to the beneficiary. Almost all of them agreed that the housing scheme is useful to the poor. It is but natural that when the poor are helped, their reaction would be appreciation of such schemes. The poor lack of knowledge of various aspects of such schemes. In a traditional society people fear that if criticisms are levelled, the schemes may be discontinued. Therefore, majority of them stated that they are thankful to the government for help.

The houseless population constitute 0.4 per cent of the total population of the State. While the houseless are 0.7 per cent of the total households in the State. The greater proportion of the houseless are in the rural areas. Of the 1,16,701 houseless persons in the State 87,775 are in the rural areas. Except Bangalore, in all the other districts the houseless population, in the rural areas exceeds that in the urban areas.

5

Socio-Economic Conditions of Rural Poor and Houseless

THAT THE housing condition includes both the physical as well as social contexts has been highlighted in the introductory chapter. The range of social and physical attributes are the salient features that should be taken into account while studying housing and its problem.

Irrespective of whether the people are houseless or live in *Janata* houses—who were till recently houseless—their economic standard of living should be studied and analysed. This fact has not been realised till recently for it was a surprise to combine the social context. It was believed that people suffer from housing problem mainly due to poverty and this could be solved by providing financial assistance to the needy. Money is not only factor in creating the housing problem, though it is one of the major factors.

This chapter deals with the economic and social life of the rural poor which includes the houseless, landless and those who are living in *Janata* houses. This is the major focus of study.

The employment opportunities, the nature of occupation, income or earnings and their material possessions are to be explained under economic context. The social life would include the type of family, authority, education, day-to-day living conditions relating to health and hygienic habits and so forth. An attempt is made to explain how housing cannot be disassociated from the development of socio-economic infrastructure. The problems, of extending this infrastructure are very many and involve huge financial commitments and technological considerations.

In the village setting a common criterion that binds everyone is the type of occupation. The financial consequences of an occupation has a direct bearing on housing amenities of people. In other words, the occupation which involves economic remuneration has a direct effect on man's life especially housing conditions.

Occupations connected with agriculture can be divided into three categories. Firstly, those who solely depend upon cultivation of land, either they cultivate the land themselves or get it cultivated through the tenants. The number of tenant cultivators has come down very much because of the recent legislation on land holding. Second group or category included those who are partly dependant on agriculture and partly engage themselves in other works. There is yet another group who are selling their labour and work on others farms.

Besides, the above categories, there are three more groups who help either in cultivation or daily living in the village. One category includes various servicing castes like the priest, smith, carpenter, potter, barber, washerman, leather worker and so forth. The mode of payment to their service is an allowance in kind at the time of harvest and some cash as well.

The second category consists of trader, the weaver, mason, oilman who are paid for specific services in cash. The third category includes village manials, servants who assist villagers. Earnings from some of these occupations these days, are very meagre. Due to increase in the village population, there is severe competition amongst those following the above occupations. Industrialisation and influence of urban life have thrown these traditional occupational groups out of jobs. Some who owned land could adjust to the changing conditions, others have migrated to cities and towns. But a large majority of rural landless have remained in village and depend on agriculture. Details are given in Table 20.

Nearly 85 per cent of the respondents are landless agricultural labourers. Working on other's land in the village. While 33.3 per cent have stated as landless, 20.8 per cent are casual workers. Those who have stated as both landless labourers as well as casual worker account for 25 per cent. There are 5.1 per cent menial workers in the study. 'Others' include occupations like smithy, carpentry, pottery etc. About 8 per cent are owner cultivators. Majority of owner cultivators also have their own houses and are included in the sample for purposes of comparative analysis.

The country is predominantly agrarian. According to the preliminary reports of 1981 census, nearly 77 per cent of the people live in villages. Majority of the Indian farmers are described as poor, illiterate, ignorant and living in debts.[1] The ratio between the rich and poor in the country is estimated in the range about 20 : 80. Less than a third of the cultivable land is under irrigation. The nature of occupation, which is dependant mainly on agriculture is seasonal. Rains or otherwise have considerable bearing on the life of people in rural areas. Any change in seasons has a direct bearing on their work. The agricultural labourers lack alternative avenues of employment. Therefore, non-availability of work for them would mean in many respects near starvation.

Manual power is the only asset of landless agricultural workers. Due to reasons beyond their control, a large number of them are without work and earnings for a good number of days in a year. Consequently, they find it very difficult to meet their basic necessities like food and clothing. Refer Table 21.

About 11 per cent of respondents get work only for less than 90 days (three months) in a year. Those who work between 150-180 days (6 months) account for another 11 per cent. Approximately 15 per cent get jobs between 120-150 and 180-210 days each. About 16 per cent have work from 90-120 days an year. One significant aspect is that about 12 per cent work between 210-240 days. Finally 9.4 per cent have job for more than 240

20. Shah, S. M. (1977), *Rural Development Planning and Reforms*, New Delhi, Abhiman Publications, p. 7.

TABLE 20

Occupation of Rural Poor and Houseless

Sl. No.	Name of the District	Landless Agricultural labour	Casual labourer	Landless Ag. Labr. & casual labourer	Menial Work	Others	Owner cultivator	Total
1.	Bangalore	110	80	100	18	22	20	350
2.	Chikmagalur	38	46	82	21	27	14	228
3.	Chitradurga	57	53	68	28	31	24	261
4.	Coorg	40	29	32	5	7	8	121
5.	Hassan	67	43	69	14	10	29	232
6.	Kolar	118	90	80	17	19	25	349
7.	Mandya	93	69	40	9	18	12	241
8.	Mysore	112	88	38	11	24	31	304
9.	Shimoga	128	62	72	8	13	17	300
10.	South Kanara	101	15	81	7	14	23	241
11.	Tumkur	110	35	90	13	17	32	297
	Total	974	610	752	151	202	235	2924
	Percentage	33.3	20.8	25.7	5.1	6.9	8.0	

TABLE 21

Number of Days Work in an Year

Sl. No.	Name of the District	Less than 90 days	Between 90-120	Between 120-150	Between 150-180	Between 180-210	Between 210-240	More than 240 days	Not Applicable owner cultivator	Total
1.	Bangalore	25	120	80	33	37	21	14	20	350
2.	Chikmagalur	30	48	41	24	31	22	17	15	228
3.	Chitradurga	21	30	46	44	40	31	19	33	261
4.	Coorg	12	15	17	11	24	18	14	10	121
5.	Hassan	27	22	20	19	44	36	29	35	232
6.	Kolar	33	47	78	45	50	42	22	32	349
7.	Mandya	20	38	40	30	35	38	21	19	241
8.	Mysore	42	43	34	25	51	40	31	38	304
9.	Shimoga	44	17	45	31	57	45	38	23	300
10.	South Kanara	27	35	20	25	35	26	45	28	241
11.	Tumkur	31	48	30	34	44	34	27	49	297
	Total	312	463	451	321	448	353	277	299	2924
	Percentage	10.6	15.8	15.4	10.9	15.3	12.0	9.4	10.2	

days in an year.

The above figures show that contrary to expectation, quite an appreciable number (37 per cent) of agricultural labourers have mentioned that they work for more than 6 months in an year. This is a basic requirement and clear indication as otherwise they have to starve. Hence, poor in the villages go in search of work that may be available readily.

In reality, each rural poor household has more than one breadwinner. Low wages force all able bodied persons and even children to undertake manual work. In some cases both husband and wife work in the fields, leaving behind small children at home. There are families where parents and even children, work in order to supplement family income. Women work during the seasons of sowing, planting, weeding and harvesting while children of ten years or less years start going for work like tending cattle, goat and sheep and otherwise assisting the farmers in agricultural operations. Refer Table 22.

In the case of 25.6 per cent of the sample families only one person works. Generally, they are men workers. About 31.4 per cent houses have two persons under agricultural labour category. Another 19.4 per cent families have three persons. Houses with four or more labourers are very few. There are about 580 (19.8 per cent) families including 235 land owning households under 'not applicable' category. These families generally work in their fields and hence are not considered as landless agricultural labourers.

Total earnings of the household comes from the labour of more than one family member. However, the income is not enough. The poor financial conditions of masses in the villages force employment of women and children under unfavourable conditions. One of the unhealthy repercussions of this situation is the problem of child labour, although, the type of occupation and the amount of earnings they get, do not enable them to spend on a good and decent housing or living.

When the income or earnings of landless labourers in villages are considered separately, it varies from region to region, from district to district and from season to season. The districts

TABLE 22

Number of Persons Working as Agricultural Labourers in each Household

Sl. No.	Name of the District	One	Two	Three	Four	Five	Six	Not Applicable	Total
1.	Bangalore	90	101	91	4	3	1	60	350
2.	Chikmagalur	69	50	39	6	2	—	62	228
3.	Chitradurga	72	60	34	4	4	2	85	261
4.	Coorg	41	32	25	2	1	—	20	121
5.	Hassan	53	70	43	6	4	3	53	232
6.	Kolar	57	125	92	9	4	1	61	349
7.	Mandya	62	92	40	5	3	—	39	241
8.	Mysore	80	96	48	8	4	2	66	304
9.	Shimoga	81	100	68	4	6	3	38	300
10.	South Kanara	62	74	53	5	3	—	44	241
11.	Tumkur	82	119	35	4	4	1	52	297
	Total	749	919	568	57	38	13	580	2924
	Percentage	25.6	31.4	19.4	1.9	1.2	0.4	19.8	

of Chikmagalur and Coorg [where there are coffee plantations, during seed plucking and pruning seasons, there will be demand for many labourers. Similarly in some taluks of Hassan, Mandya, Mysore and Shimoga districts there is irrigation. Demand for labour will be more in these areas throughout the year, especially if 3 crops are raised annually. Naturally wages will be on the higher side. But Bangalore, Kolar, Chitradurga, South Kanara and Tumkur districts have small areas under irrigation and hence demand for labour will be less and wages will also be correspondingly rather low.

Further, there is discrimination in the wages paid to men, women and children. They also vary from district to district. While the men workers get the higher rates, women are paid less and children the least. Equal wages are not paid for equal work. This kind of exploitation of the poor and helpless continue unabated under the very nose of laws provided against such discrimination.

On an average, men workers get daily wages of Rs. 5-8. Women are given between Rs. 4-6 while the child labour will earn as low a sum of Rs. 2-4, per 8 to 10 hours of work in a day. Thus their earnings are insufficient to feed all members of the household.

People get their income either as daily wages or once a week. Statutory rules like minimum wages, Act 1948 introduced in the state for the benefit of agricultural labourers have not been effective. Monthly wages system is absent. In some cases traditional annual wage system prevails. This may be either in cash or in kind. A share from the annual harvest grain mostly becomes the compensation for both the agricultural labourers and the artisan groups in the village.

Details of annual income of the respondents show that nearly 43 per cent are having earnings between 1000-2000. Another 32.7 per cent are getting less than Rs. 1000 per year. Those having annual income between Rs. 2000 and 3000 account for 13.8 per cent. Refer Table 23.

The above figures show the dismal economic conditions of the rural poor. Irregular job opportunities and low wages have

TABLE 23

Household—Annual Income

Sl. No.	Name of the District	Less than Rs. 1000	Between Rs. 1000-2000	Between Rs. 2000-3000	Between Rs. 3000-4000	Between Rs. 4000-5000	Between Rs. 5000-6000	More than Rs. 6000	No response	Total
1.	Bangalore	101	218	21	6	—	—	—	4	350
2.	Chikmagalur	88	106	18	4	9	—	—	3	228
3.	Chitradurga	121	103	24	12	1	—	—	—	261
4.	Coorg	36	58	14	8	4	—	—	1	121
5.	Hassan	62	98	45	14	8	3	—	2	232
6.	Kolar	120	169	35	12	3	2	1	7	349
7.	Mandya	61	89	65	10	5	—	—	11	241
8.	Mysore	65	158	55	16	4	4	—	2	334
9.	Shimoga	103	137	48	8	3	—	—	1	300
10.	South Kanara	75	124	32	3	2	—	—	5	241
11.	Tamkur	126	93	48	18	4	—	—	8	297
	Total	958	1353	405	111	43	9	1	44	2924
	Percentage	32.76	42.8	13.8	2.4	1.4	0.3	0.03	1.5	

adverse effect on their living conditions. When asked how are they managing with such small amount, they replied that there is no other way and are somehow pulling on.

Data relating to income and expenditure have been worked out after ascertaining details about the nature of jobs, number of persons working in each family and the average daily wages. The villagers by and large do not keep accounts. They are not aware of survey of this nature and its implications. Some respondents pleaded that their earnings are far below their family requirements and hence no use of recording it in the interview schedules.

Majority in the sample have stated that their daily wages will be spent for purchasing foodgrains and other day-to-day requirements. Only very few families have mentioned that they have stored foodgrains required for a month. Nearly 90 per cent landless agricultural labourers have hand-to-mouth existence. After the days work they are paid wages. While returning home they purchase items required for preparing meal. Reaching home, they cook daily meal and their life cycle repeats day after day.

The pattern of expenditure shows that many of the respondents are spending more than what they earn. It is natural that their income is not sufficient and hence the expenditure is usually on the higher side. Table 24 shows that those who spend Rs. 1000 or less account for 19 per cent. But nearly 32.7 per cent come under this group in annual income. Only 13.8 per cent earn Rs. 2001 to 3000 per year. Nevertheless, 30.1 per cent have said, they are spending that much annually. Families whose yearly income ranges between Rs. 3001-4000 are only 2.4 per cent in the sample, whereas nearly 12 per cent are spending this amount.

In view of the above, the poor in the village are living in a precarious condition. In order to meet any contingency they have very little or no savings. In the event of either a death or marriage they will have to borrow. Since they have no landed property, they cannot get loan easily. Alternatively, the agricultural labourers are forced to approach rural rich for help. This in turn makes them perpetually indebted, sometimes being reduced to bonded labour. Therefore, their condition cannot improve.

It is found during the study that the phenomena of poverty, underemployment, un-employment, low wages, discrimination in wages and surplus population are all simultaneously manifested in the daily life of agricultural labourers. While they get very low wages, condition of work puts an excessive burden on them and the employment which they get is extremely irregular. Further, due to poverty and indebtedness, they are under the mercy of the rural rich. This vicious circle continues and hence the problem is difficult to solve.

In the words of Mr. Pattabhi (1941) "the cultivator who spends all the days between the slush and mud, who works with a starving stomach and with half appeased appetite, who knows no rest in storm or sunshine, who other times has no dwelling site which can be called his own. He grows our paddy but starves. He feeds our milch cows but never knows beyond *ganjee* and water. . . He is perpetual hewer of wood and drawer of water for those who fatten on his labour, rise to wealth and plenty. His condition is appaling and heart rendering.[21] The situation is no better to-day.

The minimum wage policy is not effective in rural areas because of both employers unwillingness to pay and sometimes low capacity of pay and there is usually labour surplus. Therefore, the wages tend to stabilise at the subsistance level. Another reason for extremely low wages is indebtedness of workers which reduces their bargaining power and increase labour supply from the families of indebted workers. The idea of customary standard of living is deeply rooted in agriculture and there is resistance to depart from it. The system of paying wages wholly or partly in kind and giving prerequisites to workers make it difficult to assess the significance of money-wage rates.

Because of all facts mentioned above regarding the working conditions of the rural poor, we find that their income is inadequate, hence they fall a prey to debt easily. According to Pant (1970) in Indian villages, "Indebtedness is a function not of enter-

21. Mamoria, C. B. (1960), *Agricultural Problems of India*, Allahabad, Kitab Mahal, p. 71.

TABLE 24

Household—Annual Expenditure

Sl. No.	Name of the District	Less than Rs. 1000	Between Rs. 1000-2000	Between Rs. 2000-3000	Between Rs. 3000-4000	Between Rs. 4000-5000	Between Rs. 5000-6000	Between Rs. 6000-7000	No response	Total
1.	Bangalore	79	169	78	18	2	—	—	4	350
2.	Chikmagalur	45	88	86	3	2	1	—	3	228
3.	Chitradurga	74	88	68	29	1	1	—	—	261
4.	Coorg	13	42	60	5	—	—	—	1	121
5.	Hassan	29	81	103	5	8	4	—	2	232
6.	Kolar	91	132	85	25	6	3	—	7	349
7.	Mandya	23	44	88	60	10	5	1	10	241
8.	Mysore	32	120	62	78	6	4	—	2	301 (304)
9.	Shimoga	68	87	108	36	—	—	—	1	300
10.	South Kanara	43	84	63	45	1	—	—	5	241
11.	Tumkur	63	75	82	49	18	2	—	8	297
	Total	560	1010	883	353	54	20	1	43	2924
	Percentage	19.1	34.9	30.1	12.0	1.8	0.6	0.03	1.4	

prise but poverty."[3]

Debt is incurred by labourers to meet basically their daily consumptions and there is no hope of repaying that money. The rate of interest is often prohibitive property which has been amassed by a small section of rural community is not due to enterprise and efficiency or even frugality rather it is built up by the acquisition of property of small peasants. Hence, there is increase in the landless population. The poor labourers do not have any security to offer and he pledges his labour to the creditor.

Details of landed property owned by the respondents are given in Table 25.

The study consists of 134 families who owned irrigated land and about 104 (3.5 per cent) families owned garden. The owners of wet land and garden are the rural rich selected for purpose of comparative study. Hence, it is fact that the poor houseless have no land under these categories.

However, some of the respondents own dry lands. It could be seen from the table about 211 (7.2) families have less than two acres. Some 159 (5.4) families own 2-4 acres of dry lands. Those owning more than 4 acres work out 4.5 per cent (134 families).

Information regarding ownership have been verified with the village records kept with the village accountents. By and large the data tallied with the survey. Therefore, it is true that the poor are also landless. Those who are houseless are the families who occupy the lowest position among the poor and the landless. Their living conditions are precarious and cannot be easily imagined.

The survey enumerated details of possessions of the respondents like domestic animals, agricultural implements, furniture and radio or transistors and so on.

As many as 2588 (88.5 per cent) families have said that they keep poultry. But this is not to infer that it is done on large scale, definitely not as an industry. As observed at the time of field work, generally one or two birds are reared by them. The respondents humourously remarked that they will be cooked whenever there is an occasion like visit of relatives or festivals. About 614 (20.9 per

---

2. Pant, S. C. (1970), *Indian Labour Problem*, Allahabad, Chaitanya Publishing House, p. 383.

TABLE 25

Landed Assets

(*in acres*)

Sl. No.	Name of the District	Wet land			Dry land			Garden		
		0-2	2-4	More than 4	0-2	2-4	More than 4	0-2	2-4	More than 4
1.	Bangalore	—	—	1	25	14	1	—	—	—
2.	Chikmagalur	—	—	3	10	9	3	—	—	—
3.	Chitradurga	—	2	3	25	19	5	3	1	1
4.	Coorg	—	1	2	11	9	3	—	—	2
5.	Hassan	1	6	3	29	18	10	6	2	2
6.	Kolar	4	5	11	28	17	20	14	3	3
7.	Mandya	6	12	9	16	11	27	15	8	4
8.	Mysore	2	2	3	21	15	7	4	3	—
9.	Shimoga	5	6	6	13	14	17	2	3	4
10.	South Kanara	10	4	3	8	12	17	6	2	1
11.	Tumkur	7	10	7	25	21	24	8	4	3
	Total	35	48	51	211	159	134	58	26	20
	Percentage	1.9	1.6	1.7	7.2	5.4	4.6	1.9	0.8	0.7
	Total		134(4.5)			504(17.2)			104(3.5)	
	Not applicable		2790(95.4)			2420(82.7)			2820(96.4)	
	Total		2924			2924			2924	

cent) families kept one or two sheep. Again they have stated that these are reared usually for sacrificing at the time of village deity festivals. Majority of them have mentioned, they have a vow to fulfil to local God or Goddess and hence they kept them. Normally these sheep will be reared for about eight to ten months before they are sacrificed.

Nearly 1021 (34.9 per cent) families possessed pigs. Majority have said that they got government assistance and therefore are able to keep them. It is a fact that in villages, money is being distributed to the weaker sections of the society, especially to SCs and STs to purchase pigs. But what is happening is that rearing pig carries stigma in the villages and it is being perpetuated indirectly. As usual SC/ST families in the sample have one or two pigs while the other castes though houseless and poor never utilised this benefit.

Majority in the sample do not possess cattle and carts. This is natural because when they have no land and house they see no purpose in owning them. Further, cattle and cart cost more money. The economic conditions of the poor will not permit to own cattle and cart. The 112 (3.8 per cent) and 134 (4.5 per cent) families who own cattle and carts respectively, are the rural rich with landed property and these are included in the sample survey.

There are 332 (11.3 per cent) families in the study who own a bicycle or watch. A large number of them are the land owning families and those living in *Janata* houses. While the bicycles are the popular mode of transport, watches are status symbols in village society. But a large number in the study do not possess them. This indicates that the poor are not in a position to purchase some of these items during their life time.

Items like furniture, radio or transistor are also seen only in the houses of rural rich and those living in *Janata* houses. Very often furniture at home, would be a cot, chair, stool and table made out of wood. Very rarely the survey recorded steel furniture.

Compared to the popularity of radio and transistor, the poor are not able to have such items of entertainment. The cost of radio and transistors, though have come down recently, are not within the reach of the poor in the village. Besides, even this item is a prestigious possession in the rural parts of Karnataka, hence the poor cannot own them.

The problems of the poor and houseless are linked with the problem of economic development. Remedies lie in bringing about fundamental changes in the agrarian structure and social relationships in the rural setting. The difficulty with agriculture is that tradition plays an important role and it is carried on under the conditions of surplus manpower.

The long neglected and exploited poor agricultural workers from the most vulnerable section of our society need urgent attention and early solution, if not out of the sympathy for the poor toiling labourers, but at least with a view to ward off the danger of social tensions of increasing dimensions.

Increase in agricultural production and productivity, expansion of economic opportunities, redistribution of land, provision of better social overheads and building up improved infrastructure are all aspects of an integrated approach to the problems of agricultural labourers. Like industrial working force, they have also to be assisted, guided and led in the right perspective in furtherance of their own as well as national interests.[4]

By and large the family, among the rural houseless and the *Janata* households consists of husband, wife and their children. Very rarely parents of the head of the households live with them. Due to grinding poverty many cannot afford to maintain the old and the infirm and therefore their number in the sample households is very negligible. Only in about 114 families grand parents and grand children are living together.

A general trend observed during field work is that respondents thought that the investigator must be government officials and the details are being asked to extend the benefits in the near future. Therefore, family of each married sons and daughters were given separate identity. Their anxiety was to get benefit to each of their

---

4. Carl C. Taylor (S) (1965), *India's Roots of Democracy*, Bombay Orient Longmans, p. 29.

family members separately. Such is the magnitude of the housing problem in villages.

The three major components of Indian society traditionally consisted of family, caste and village community. Among them, the joint family has undergone rapid changes at present. It has disintegrated among the rural people, especially among the rural houseless. The model named 'traditional Hindu Joint Family' is absent among them but is seen among a few rural affluents. The small family though regarded as an urban phenomenon is prevalent in villages. The functional side of the family also revolves in a circle consisting of the parents and children. This family is an independent entity embracing the roles of bread-winning, household management and adjustment to a new kind of life outside the family. Though its size is small when compared with the traditional joint family, the members are numerically more. The houseless have at least 4-5 children per household. Hence, the condition is that the small house accommodates the larger family. The size of the family and the size of the house do not correspond with one another. Demographically speaking, there is overcrowding in the houses.

Normally, male members hold authority in every household. Women and children are under the control of husband and father. The society is male dominated. Though women and children work equally and contribute to the fomily earnings, father is given the authority to control the family functioning. The worst affected are the women and children who overwork. Women usually attend to cooking and household work, in addition they also work on others' lands as *coolies*.

Unlike traditional families in these households women and children enjoy some liberty. The women go out for shopping, children have opportunity early in their life to participate in family economy and other social responsibility.

Not only the economy but also illiteracy of these houseless rural masses add to the poor housing condition. Among the houseless and *Janata* house residents in the sample, not even a single family has a person who has obtained Bachelors's degree. Those who went to college are negligible. There are about 108 households where one person has completed matriculation. High illiteracy among children and adults is prevalent and many children leave school before reaching the fourth standard and often students from these households stay more than one year in one class.

There is an increasing rate of drop-outs from schools inspite of incentives given for education. The rural people face the problems of lack of basic education facilities for young children. High illiteracy added with ignorance have resulted in the creation of prejudice against formal education. Though the constitution of India declared compulsory free primary education, this does not in any way bring out any reduction in the rate of illiteracy for various reasons.

The poor in villages are also unaware of nutrition and its value to healthy body. Their hygienic practices have created unhealthy conditions leading to diseases. Their staple food consists mostly of *ragi* (millet) and rice. While vegetables are sparingly used, the diet is lacking in vitamins and proteins largely. Meat tends to be a luxury but still they take it occasionally. Hence, when the question of nutrition comes, it is a casualty and therefore the poor villagers are prone to various diseases. The health hazards in rural parts are also caused by lack of proper medical facilities, lack of proper hygienic environment viz., safe drinking water supply and sanitation, low resistance due to lack of balanced diet and poor nutrition, general and health education and proper housing.

On the whole, the rural houseless economically, socially, educationally and physically, do not enjoy the benefits out of anything. No doubt, the housing shortage among them has been for long, but during the last 50 years or so it has assumed enormous proportions due to the combined effect of a multiplicity of factors, like rapid increase in the population, breakdown of the age-old joint-family system especially significant in the context of housing, slow rate of construction of new houses . . . very rapidly adding to the already existing backlong of an alarming magnitude of our housing stock. To these should be added the politicisation of the various programmes especially housing, the role of intermediaries, economics of the programme and the role of government officials. Everything is interlinked both directly and indirectly. A change in one should be viewed to produce chain reaction in all others. As Professor Madan has rightly put it that difficulties are involved in rapid economic development in the underdeveloped countries—these difficulties are of vide range including economic, social, legal, religious and political factors.[24] The self-realisation about the seriousness and severity of the problem by all who are related with it, would assure the success of any programme.

---

24. Madan, G.R. (1976), *Indian Social Problem*, Vol. I, Allied Publishers, New Delhi.

6

Planned Rural Housing in Karnataka

THE TOTAL population of Karnataka in 1981 was 37,135,714. About 76 per cent (26,406,108) of the States population live in rural areas.[1] There are about 26,826 villages in the State. Out of 6,263,687 occupied houses, 4,461,876 are in villages.[2] Approximately 80 per cent of the houses are used for residential purposes.

It was estimated that during 1971, the State had 17,16,110 landless agricultural labourers and the number of house-sites required in rural areas was about 9 lakhs. This figure may go up due to population growth and splitting of joint-families. Hence, the problem is a complex one and very difficult to solve in the near future.

The Ministry of Works and Housing, Government of India as early as in 1971 initiated a programme to be implemented on priority, to provide house-sites to the landless and siteless families in rural areas. Accordingly, all the State Governments were requested to take up the issues with a sense of urgency. Under the scheme,

---

1. Census of India 1981, General Population tables, Government of India, New Delhi, 1985.

2. Government of Karnataka, Bureau of Economics and Statistics, "Karnataka at a Glance 1971", Bangalore.

proposals for village extension were received from the Deputy Commissioners and acquisition proceedings launched. In addition, the social welfare department in the State had separate plans for acquisition of land to provide house-sites to SCs, STs, Denotified Tribes, Nomadic and Semi-nomadic Tribes.

The Government of India have introduced yet another scheme during 1972. Under this scheme, families of landless workers who do not own a site or a house or a hut on the lands of their own will be provided with house-sites. The scheme was fully assisted by the Central Government. The State Government implemented the scheme and was planning to distribute about 3 lakh house-sites over a period of five years starting from 1972. The programme gave top priority to give house-sites to the landless labour and SCs in a phased manner. Each year at least one lakh sites have to be provided covering at least one-fifth of the number of village in a Taluk. However, the Deputy Commissioners were given powers to implement the scheme by covering more villages.

Land required for providing house-sites to landless and SCs will utilise the available government land or *Gomala* (Village common cattle grazing ground). In the event of non-availability of such land, it may be obtained by donations from philanthropic villagers. It was also provided for acquisition of suitable land under the Land Acquisition Act. However, lands of SCs and Tribal people were exempted from acquisition for the purpose. While selecting the village in the first instance, preference should be given to places with a high school, primary health centre or a shandy.

A committee consisting of Tahsildar, Block Development Officer (Convenor), Officer-in-charge of Primary Health Centre and Social Welfare Inspector will select the land required, in consultation with the village panchayats. Certain guidelines were given in this regard in that the land selected for acquisition should be non-controversial to avoid delay in acquisition as far as possible. Private lands must be secured on the basis of private transactions available locally preferably on the lines of Trust Board Act. The area of the land should not be less than 150 square yards. The location must be nearer to the village and working place of the prospective allottees. The land selected should be suitable from hygienic point of view. The Assistant Commissioner must supervise the work. The unit for formulation of the project shall be the Community Development Block.

To avoid delay in acquisition a time schedule had to be worked out giving minimum possible time under the law. Where sites are allotted out of available government land or *gomala*, the process should be completed within three months of the issue of the Government Order. Similarly proposals for notification under Land Acquisition Act, should be sent to government through revenue department within a period of three months. The Deputy Commissioners will review the progress at the monthly meetings of the District Co-ordination Committee. The Divisional Commissioners, based on the reports will inspect the progress of the scheme from time to time.

Lands acquired for the purpose will be developed as per the models given by the State Housing Board depending on the number of sites. Under the scheme, provision is also made for planting two coconut trees in every house-site.

To encourage philanthropic people to denote lands for the purpose of colonies, it was decided to name the area after them or as suggested by them. The present scheme is a composite one which includes SCs, STs and other landless families irrespective of castes and communities. It was believed that the scheme would ensure the development of extensions, consisting of rural families of all categories and sections of the village society.

During the years 1972-73 and 1973-74, the scheme of distribution of free sites in rural areas was financed by the central government and then 1974-75 onwards, the scheme was financed out of the state plan provisions. In the year 1975-76 this was included as one of the points in the twenty point economic programme.

As on October, 1978 about 8.79 lakh rural families in the State were identified as site-less. Among them 7.93 lakh families represented weaker sections and therefore most of them were given free sites.

The following figures indicate the year-wise break-up of

distribution of the house-sites in the State :

Sl. No.	*Year*	*No. of Sites distributed*
1.	1972-73	2,33,888
2.	1973-74	50,784
3.	1974-75	49,639
4.	1975-76	3,01,032
5.	1976-77	1,10,186
6.	1977-78	42,424
	Total	7,87,953

The percentage of SCs and STs who were allotted house-site works out to 36.0.

Normally the programme is financed out of plan provisions. However, the State Government is spending more money for acquiring lands and to improving them. Various development departments in the State are incharge of providing approach road, drinking water, electricity and sanitation to the new colony. It is said that nearly 4.0 crores of rupees have already been spent on the scheme. Details of annual expenditure are given below :

Sl. No.	*Year*	*Amount spent (Rs. in Lakhs)*
1.	1972-73	21.03
2.	1973-74	54.53
3.	1974-75	40.96
4.	1975-76	101.69
5.	1976-77	90.92
6.	1977-78	46.00
7.	1978-79	50.00

The Government made it obligatory on the part of Revenue Officers in the district to conduct periodical checks of the distribution of sites and verify whether the physical possession of the sites has been actually given and also to ascertain whether the sites allotted are suitable. Details of inspection responsibility are as follows :

Sl. No.	*Officers*	*Percentage of sites to be test-checked*
1.	Divisional Commissioners	2
2.	Deputy Commissioners	5
3.	Assistant Commissioners	10
4.	Block Development Officers	33

People's Housing Scheme

Recognising the magnitude of the problem of housing of the poor and the downtrodden, the State Government during 1973-74 launched a low-cost housing scheme. The people's housing scheme, popularly known as 'Janata Housing Scheme' is a follow-up of the programme of distribution of house-sites exclusively for the weaker sections in the villages.

Some of the main features of this scheme are novel. Each house with an estimated cost of Rs. 2,500 will be built by the government or the beneficiary must take up construction. Out of the estimated cost of Rs. 2,500, Rs. 1,000 is given as interest-free loan. Another sum of Rs. 1,000 is treated as subsidy. The remaining Rs. 500 will have to be borne by the allottees either in the form of cash or labour.

The plinth area of the house varies between 200 to 250 sq. ft. Repayment of loan amount by monthly instalments works out of Rs. 4 approximately. Details of type design and other specifications have taken note of the rainfall, climate and the construction practices prevailing in different regions of the State. A technical committee under the Chairmanship of the Chief Engineer (Construction and Building) has been guiding the design aspects. After 1976—some changes are effected in designs and specifications because of the escalation in cost of construction.

Technical information regarding specifications and the recommended building layout are enclosed as Annexure A-I.

Another scheme called 'The experimental low cost housing' was introduced during 1976. In this scheme, each beneficiary will be given roof materials, doors and windows costing about Rs. 1,000. In addition, the allottee is sanctioned Rs. 250 in two instalments to meet the construction charges. He is expected to construct the surrounding walls on his own. The total financial assistance of Rs. 1,250 is treated as subsidy. One of the main idea behind the scheme is that even when the surrounding walls collapse, the roofs should remain pucca and the walls could be rebuilt when the economic condition improves.

To cover the housing need of the poorest among the weaker sections who are not in a position to contribute their share under the other schemes, another scheme was introduced during 1976. This is known as construction of huts scheme. In this case materials worth Rs. 250 are supplied to each family and the beneficiary is expected to complete the hut with his own labour. The area of the hut is 180 sq. ft. The reason for promoting this scheme was to have wider coverage of population in view of its low cost and to enable the weakest to have minimum temporary shelter. During 1978 only low priority is given to hutment scheme.

The three schemes—Peoples' Housing Scheme, Experimental Low Cost Housing Scheme and the Hutment Scheme are restricted to rural areas of the State. Further the beneficiary must be houseless and have an income not exceeding Rs. 2,000 per annum. Certain of the priorities for allotment of the houses are as follows :

1. All the families of Nomadic, Semi-nomadic notified and Denotified Tribes in the State.
2. Scheduled Castes.
3. Scheduled Tribes.
4. Minorities—namely; Muslims, Buddhists, Jains and Christians.
5. Ex-servicemen, Defence Personnel in Service, Political Sufferers.

6. Backward classes who are socially, economically and educationally backward.
7. Other sections.

Normally, the beneficiaries are the allottees under the house-sites-programme.

Figures below indicate the number of houses and huts completed till 1978 in the State.

Name of the series	*Year of completion*	*No. of houses completed to end of Aug. 1978*
Peoples' Housing Scheme		
I Series	1973-74	14,377
II Series	1974-75	20,907
III Series	1975-76	16,893
IV Series	1976-77	21,646
V Series	1977-78	14,138
VI Series	1978-79	396
Total		88,357
Experimental Low Cost Housing Scheme		
I Series	1976-77	8,664
II Series	1977-78	8,009
III Series	1978-79	130
Total		16,803
Hutment Scheme		
I Series	1976-77	24,609
II Series	1977-78	10,512
III Series	1978-79	110
Total		35,231
Grand Total		1,40,391

Out of 1,40,391 dwellings, more than half have been allotted to the members of Scheduled Castes and Scheduled Tribes.

A budget provision of Rs. 10 crores have been made during the year 1978-79 out of which a sum of Rs. 5 crores has been released towards the People's Housing Scheme. The remaining sum of Rs. 5 crores is set apart as the matching share (subsidy portion) of State Government to avail the sanctioned loan of Rs. 5 crores from the HUDCO. From the total outlay of Rs. 150 crores ,it is expected that about 75,000 houses would be constructed during the year 1978-79.

Schemes Under Karnataka Housing Board

The State Government constituted a Housing Board as a statutory body effective from 1-6-1956. This board has been constructing houses under various housing schemes for general public in all the districts of Karnataka. The following are the schemes taken up by the Board since its inception.

Integrated housing schemes for industrial workers and economically weaker sections of the community :

1. (*a*) Subsidised Industrial Housing Scheme (State and Employer Sectors).
   (*b*) Subsidised Rental Housing Scheme.
   (*c*) Economically Weaker Sections Housing Scheme.
2. Low Income Group Housing Scheme.
3. Middle Income Group Housing Scheme.
4. Rental Housing Scheme for Low Paid Government Employees, KHB employees, Teachers, Village-accountants and Para-medical staff.
5. Rural Housing Scheme.

Finance is provided by the State Government under the plan allocation. To augment the funds, loans are obtained from Life Insurance Corporation of India through the State Government. To meet the heavy commitments, the board has also been raising debenture loans. A brief account of various housing schemes of the board is given here.

The integrated subsidised housing scheme for industrial workers and the subsidised rental housing scheme for economically weaker sections under low income group housing schemes have been integrated into one scheme with a uniform pattern of State plan assistance. The subsidized industrial housing scheme is taken up both under State sector and employer's sector. Projects taken under State sectors are directly executed by the Karnataka Housing Board. Projects taken up under employer's sector are implemented by the employers for whom cash loan assistance is given to construct tenements to their industrial workers. The maximum period of repayment is 25 years.

The subsidised industrial housing scheme assistance for the construction of houses for labour is provided under the state plan. Those who are eligible for assistance under the scheme are :

1. Workers within the meaning of section 2 (1) of the Factories Act, 1948 as amended from time to time.
2. Those employed in mines other than coal and mica mines within the meaning of section 2 (h) of the Mines Act, 1952 as amended from time to time.

Progress made under the schemes is shown below :

Sl. No.	*Year*	*No. of Houses completed*	*Amount spent (Rs. in lakhs)*
1.	1974-75	260	12.27
2.	1975-76	285	38.12
3.	1976-77	318	52.00
	Total	863	102.39

The houses constructed under low income group housing scheme are allotted to eligible individuals whose annual income does not exceed Rs. 7,200. The Board has already constructed and allotted houses in all the districts of the state. As when the houses are ready, applications are invited from the public by notification in the newspapers and houses are disposed of on lease-cum-sale basis according to the allotment regulations of the Board. Details of houses constructed are as follows:

Sl. No.	*Year*	*No. of houses constructed*	*Amount spent (Rs. in lakhs)*
1.	1974-75	400	24.17
2.	1975-76	342	101.66
3.	1976-77	254	82.32
	Total	996	208.15

The Board is constructing houses under middle income group housing scheme. Individuals whose annual income is between Rs. 7,200 and Rs. 18,000 are eligible houses constructed as mentioned hereunder are allotted to members of the public.

Sl. No.	*Year*	*No. of houses constructed*	*Amount spent (Rs. in lakhs)*
1.	1974-75	87	11.36
2.	1975-76	35	32.50
3.	1976-77	46	19.54
	Total	168	63.40

Under the rental housing scheme, the Karnataka Housing Board is constructing quarters for the low paid government employees at all Taluks of the State. At least 12 tenements are being planned in each Taluk headquarters. The construction is taken up on behalf of the State Government and the amount spent on these quarters will be repaid by the government. Details of the progress under the scheme are as follows :

Sl. No.	*Year*	*No. of houses constructed*	*Amount spent (Rs. in lakhs)*
1.	1974-75	130	7.09
2.	1975-76	201	8.38
3.	1976-77	297	7.89
	Total	628	23.36

Rural housing scheme was previously under the administrative control of Rural Development and Co-operation Department of the State Government. During 1970, the same was transferred to Karnataka Housing Board. The following particulars are relevant regarding implementation of the scheme :

Sl. No.	*Year*	*No. of houses constructed*	*Amount spent (Rs. in lakhs)*
1.	1974-75	1625	65.63
2.	1975-76	611	62.70
3.	1976-77	1554	57.61
	Total	3790	185.94

During 1977-78 and 1978-79 the board concentrated on the incomplete work. Fresh construction for the benefit of economically weaker sections and low income group has been taken up mainly to overcome the regional imbalance in the development of housing in the State.

Following are the scheme-wise details for 1977-78 and 1978-79.

(Rs. in lakhs)

Sl. No.	*Scheme*	*1977-78*		*1978-79*	
		No. of houses	*Amount spent*	*No. of houses*	*Amount spent*
1.	Integrated subsidised housing scheme				
	(*a*) Subsidised industrial housing scheme	284	24.65	280	26.00
	(*b*) Subsidised rental housing scheme	600	20.00	800	35.00
	(*c*) Economically weaker section housing scheme	300	20.00	475	30.00
2.	Low income group housing scheme	400	46.00	530	59:00
3.	Middle income group housing scheme	100	21.00	60	10.00
4.	Rental housing scheme, quarters for low paid government employees	203	29.00	379	39.00
5.	Rural housing scheme	2000	68.85	4400	101.00

TABLE 26

Rural Houseless and Peoples Housing 1978

Sl. No.	*District*	*No. of villages*	*Rural population*	*No. of houseless families*	*No. of houses built upto 1978*
1.	Bangalore	2470	1499761	29496	19042
2.	Belgaum	1158	1943887	38877	24682
3.	Bellary	589	817914	16357	10383
4.	Bidar	591	704928	14099	8950
5.	Bijapur	1245	1564216	31284	19860
6.	Chikmagalur	1110	621569	12428	7892
7.	Chitradurga	1478	259706	22285	13850
8.	Coorg	291	319600	6393	4058
9.	Dharwar	1337	1604240	32085	27517
10.	Gulbarga	1304	1429944	28600	18155
11.	Hassan	2576	952959	19054	12098
12.	Kolar	2828	1103531	22070	14008
13.	Mandya	1339	489652	9794	6216
14.	Mysore	1592	1548128	30962	19656
15.	North Kanara	1295	698608	13971	8866
16.	Raichur	1364	1198269	23966	15212
17.	Shimoga	1728	994172	19884	12623
18.	South Kanara	663	1546137	30919	19574
19.	Tumkur	2728	1437114	28737	18245
	Total	27686	20734335	431261	280887

Sources : (1) Information in columns No. 1 and 2 is obtained from Karnataka at a glance—from Bureau of Economics and Statistics in Karnataka.

(2) Details of houseless families and the No. of houses built under various rural housing scheme are from various Block Development Offices in the State.

The study included 1264 *Janata* sample houses. As explained earlier at the time of selecting respondents in villages equal weightage was given to both houseless population and those living in *Janata* houses. The residents of *Janata* houses were till recently houseless. In fact one of the main criteria to obtain *Janata* houses is that, the beneficiary must not have owned any house or land. In other words, *Janata* houses are given to the poorest of the poor in villages.

Peoples' houses under various schemes, are built on the outskirts of the village on lands acquired for the said purpose. They are constructed in clusters of 10-20 houses which look almost like a separate colony. Each house has a plinth area of approximately 200-250 sq ft. It has a hall and a small kitchen. The roof is usually covered by tiles and reeds. However, not much skill is needed in the construction of the houses.

The policy of the government is to encourage mixed housing in villages. This is getting favourable response from the rural people. People of different religious denomination and various caste groups live in *Janata* houses. However, in some villages all the *Janata* houses are given to scheduled castes and tribes.

Religious composition of the sample households indicate that all the three major religious groups—Hindus, Muslims, and Christians—live in *Janata* houses. Most of the sample districts have Muslims and Christians living with Hindus.

A large majority of the respondents (83.8 per cent) have felt that it is desirable that all caste and religious groups live intermixed. Many feel that such housing colonies encourage co-operation (34.4 per cent) among different communities in the villages. About 24.5 per cent have stated that such colonies bring social integration among various groups and in some cases (22.7 per cent) even reforms the lower caste persons. However, the 13.9 per cent who did not favour this proposition have felt that such attempts will result in intercaste rivalry and hence must be discouraged. There are a number of persons who consider that the present pattern of segregated housing must continue.

Scheduled castes and tribes are given preference in the allotment of *Janata* houses. Compared to other caste, Hindu communities, the SCs/STs are poor and landless. Therefore, they are the most eligible and deserve a roof to live under. Accordingly 52.1 per cent respondents have said that SCs/STs live in *Janata* houses. Another 32.8 per cent expressed that poor and houseless poor of all castes live in *Janata* houses.

The average number of members in each *Janata* household works out to five. The living space available to them is not sufficient. By and large, the houses they live are single room dwellings. There is no privacy for elders and children. All the members have to sleep in the small space available. They have to keep their pets, domestic animals and birds along with them during nights. There is no other place to store their belongings.

The present accommodation is not sufficient to a large number (67.0 per cent) of them. They are somehow managing by squeezing in the available space. Only 19.4 per cent of respondents have stated that it is sufficient. They felt that in the absence of roof to live under, they are insecure. However, they have agreed that it is necessary to keep domestic animals separately otherwise people living in *Janata* houses are exposed to health-hazards. Nearly 7.6 per cent have 'no opinion' on this point.

The principal aim of *Janata* housing scheme is to provide one of the basic necessities. In order to discourage abuse of the benefit, certain restrictions are put on the beneficiary. The allottees of *Janata* houses are not permitted to sell, sub-divide, mortgage, exchange, or let out the house for rent. Though majority (66.8 per cent) of the beneficiary are not violating the rules, there are instances where people were successful in subverting the rules of allotment. In the sample households, thirty respondents have stated that they can sell their houses in case of need. As many as 144 respondents have sub-divided their houses, while 93 persons have expressed that they can mortgage. About 31 households have said that they can exchange and while nearly 124 respondents have indicated the possibility of letting out their houses. Details of opinion about mortgage and subletting are given in Table 27.

The *Janata* houses are built a bit away from the main village.

TABLE 27

Janata Houses Can Be

Sl. No.	*Name of the District*	*Sold*	*Sub-divided*	*Mort-gaged*	*Exchang-ed*	*Let out*	*No*	*Total*
1.	Bangalore	1	19	10	1	9	129	169
2.	Chikmagalur	2	20	12	—	15	103	152
3.	Chitradurga	5	18	8	2	11	93	137
4.	Coorg	1	9	6	2	8	58	84
5.	Hassan	3	12	11	3	12	69	110
6.	Kolar	6	18	12	5	17	76	134
7.	Mandya	1	8	7	4	7	61	88
8.	Mysore	—	6	4	2	8	50	70
9.	Shimoga	4	13	9	6	14	77	123
10.	South Kanara	4	11	8	4	13	70	110
11.	Tumkur	3	10	6	2	10	56	87
	Total	30	144	93	31	124	842	1264
	Percentage	2.27	11.39	7.35	2.45	9.81	66.61	

They lack many basic amenities like proper approach roads, electricity, water, sanitation, postal services, school and health services.

In the sample villages, the *Janata* houses are not having proper water facilities. Only in seven villages, the colonies had separate tube wells. They have to depend upon village common wells and tanks which are usually far away. There are some villages with tap-water facilities But the *Janata* houses in such villages are, however, not provided with taps.

Only about 15.5 per cent *Janata* houses are having electricity connections. The rest use kerosene lamps. While the main village has street lights, the newly formed *Janata* housing colonies have no street-lights. Only recently the State government has approved the provision for free electric connections to SCs/STs living in *Janata* houses. But details of implementation of government scheme are not readily available.

Children coming from *Janata* households go to village schools and there is no problem with regard to education of children in the villages. But about 14.4 per cent respondents have stated that there is no school in the village and hence their children have no education.

Almost 94 per cent of people living in *Janata* households have stated that postal services are available to them. The 6.3 per cent who are not getting postal services are cases where the village is not having Post office and it is attached to a distant Post office.

A large number of *Janata* house respondents, 92.4 per cent are not having any health services. By and large, the villages have no hospitals and therefore the question of health facilities does not arise.

Majority of the *Janata* housing colonies (92.4 per cent) have no proper roads. Only about 7.7 per cent have somewhat proper roads. Since laying of all-weather roads involve large expenditure, the village panchayats cannot afford to spend money for road building. Details of civic facilities are given in Table 28.

TABLE 28
Services Available to Houses

Sl. No.	Name of the District	Tape Water supply		Domestic electric connection		School of children		Postal services		Health services		Roads	
		Yes	No	Yes	No	Yes	No	Yes	No	Yes	No	Yes	No
1.	Bangalore	—	169	20	149	161	8	161	8	8	161	2	167
2.	Chikmagalur	—	152	12	140	140	12	150	2	2	150	4	148
3.	Chitradurga	—	137	19	118	120	17	132	5	5	132	7	130
4.	Coorg	—	84	8	76	55	29	74	10	3	81	6	78
5.	Hassan	—	110	15	95	88	22	101	9	10	100	8	102
6.	Kolar	—	134	41	93	120	14	124	10	8	126	13	121
7.	Mandya	—	88	14	74	60	28	80	8	7	81	10	78
8.	Mysore	—	70	10	60	50	20	60	10	10	60	9	61
9.	Shimoga	—	123	40	83	118	5	120	3	24	99	20	103
10.	South Kanara	—	110	10	100	102	8	102	8	14	96	8	102
11.	Tumkur	—	87	7	80	67	20	80	7	7	80	8	79
	Total		1264	196	1068	1081	183	1184	80	98	1166	95	1169
	Percentage			15.5	84.4	85.5	14.4	93.6	6.3	7.7	92.2	7.5	92.4

7

Land Reforms and Rural Houseless

INDIA HAS been a predominantly agricultural country. Nearly 70 per cent of the population is engaged in agriculture and this generates over 50 per cent of the country's national income. It is said that the farmers constitute under-privileged and get lower average incomes than are enjoyed by non-farming sections. The rural population has increased steadily over the past few decades resulting in pressure on land. Side by side, the agricultural labourers have increased more rapidly than the agricultural population as a whole. To the extent these two trends prevail, a larger percentage of the rural population closer to the bottom of the agricultural workers are becoming landless and an increasing percentage of land owners are being compelled to eke out a living on extremely small holdings. Further, the vast majority of the cultivating households do not have enough cultivable land, sufficient working capital or credit or indeed the technical know-how to obtain higher yields on land they tilled.[1] The agrarian economy and the conditions of agricultural workers in India and how deplorable becomes clear from the above description.

1. Tylor, C., *et. al.* (1955), *India's Report of Democracy*, New Delhi, Orient Longmans, pp. 122-123.

Land tenurial institutions are of most importance in determining the course of economic development. They explain the relationship of the cultivator with the land. In the words of Philip Raup 'Land tenure institutions define a farmer's status.' They create the framework of expectations within which hopes and fears motivate him to economic activity. Land tenure system in India existed even during early period. The king held land in his name though he did not exercise any property-right on land. The land was held by the cultivators who could not alienate it. The king's customary share was one-sixth to one-fourth of the produce which was known as customary 'pargana'. In certain parts of India namely Punjab, U.P., M.P. and in South India, all village lands were jointly held by village communities.[2] In the Muslim period there was a revival of trade and expansion of money economy. The character of the land system underwent radical change during the British period. The state exercised supremacy over the land. The system of fixed payment in cash replaced the traditional share of the government in the produce paid by the village communities as a whole.

During the British rule three types of land ownership were divised. In 1793, the British East India Company converted the farmers and revenue collectors into private landlords, granting for some the right of private property in land. This was done so that the land would bring greatly enhanced revenues to the state. This type of land tenure came to be known as the Zamindari system. Later, the British Government, introduced the *Ryotwari* system of land tenure in the South which was again intended to realise more revenues. Under the system, each peasant was recognised as holding a particular plot or plots, he cultivated but his right to land depended upon the annual payment of money-rent in full to the state, which was rather heavy. Under the Mahalwari system, the villagers concerned were units by themselves and the ownership of the property was by the community as a whole.

Because of the Zamindari and Ryotwari system, the problem

2. Shah, S.M. (1977), *Rural Development, Planning and Reforms*. New Deihi, Abhiman Publications, p. 74.

of tenancy in the country assumed great importance. The high rents paid by the farmers nearly destroyed all incentives to improve farms and farming methods. Besides, there were gross inequalities in land ownership. According to Voelcker "a defective land system is one of the causes of low productivity of agriculture in India.[3] In the words of S.C. Jain, the system of land tenure is the pivot round which all other agricultural problems revolve. He further observed that the land ownership has been so radically affected and led to such complex variety of tenures and tenants that apart from their economic inadequacy, the peasants everywhere came to be degraded into slavery, serfdom and peonage.[4]

Independence paved the way for the enactment of different legislative measures for improving the condition of tenants who were a prey to the whims and fancies of intermediaries. It was felt that a radical change is essential in the prevailing land tenure system. As suggested by the Congress Agrarian Reforms Committee 1949, land reforms was implemented by the Government of India.

Broadly, land reforms have been undertaken on the following lines.[5]

1. Abolition of intermediary or Zamindari rights.
2. Tenancy legislation aimed at reduction of rent, security of tenure and purchase of land by tenants.
3. Ceiling on individual holdings and distribution of surplus-land among the landless.
4. Co-operative farming and co-operative management.

The cornerstone of tenancy reforms in India is the acceptance of the principle that land must belong to the tiller. The government policy behind tenancy reforms is 'to put a complete end to

---

3. Voelcker, A. J., (1893), Report on the Improvement of Agriculture, p. 289.

4. Jain, S. C. (1967), *Agricultural Policy in India,* Delhi, Allied Publishers Ltd., p. 115.

5. Nanavati, M. B. and Anjaria, J. J., (1970), *The Indian Rural Problem*, Bombay, [Indian Society of Agricultural Economics, p. 250.

the landlord-tenant nexus and to convert tenants into full owners'.[6]

After considering, in brief, the evolution of land reforms in the country, let us turn to know the trend in Karnataka before evaluating how these reforms have not reached the rural poor and houseless.

The *Ryotwari* system is in vogue in the South and land tenures are broadly divided into two categories viz., *Sarkar* or Government lands and *Inam* (gift) lands. Government lands were mainly held under the *Ryotwari* tenure, the assessment in most cases being subject to revision once in 30 years. An *Inam*—a village or portion of the village— is a grant by government for the personal benefit of individual or individuals or for religious, charitable and other purposes or for meritorious services rendered to the state. *Inams* are usually free of assessment or at the best subject to light assessment (Jodi).

In August, 1948, the then State Government (Mysore Government) appointed a committee for the revision of the land revenue system following a persistent demand from the public and also in both the houses of State legislature. The committee's recommendations included the following :

> "To consider the feasibility of simplifying land tenures by the abolition of Jodi, Inam and Jahagir tenures and to recommend the principles for the payment of fair compensation in respect of each class."[7]

First the State Government enacted the Mysore Alienated Villages (Protection of Tenants and Miscellaneous Provisions) Act; which seeks to protect the right of tenants pending the abolition of Inams. Following this the Mysore Government passed the Inam Village (Abolition of Inam Tenure) Bill, 1951 for the abolition of Inam tenure throughout the state.

---

6. Shah, S. M., (1977), *Rural Development Planning Reforms*, New Delhi, Abhiman Publishers, pp. 78-79.

7. Malaviya, H. V. (1954), *Land Reforms in India*, Calcutta, Sri Gouranga Press, p. 45.

Again in 1952, pursuant to the recommendations by the Mysore Land Revenue Reforms Committee 1950, the Government passed the Mysore Tenancy Act in 1952. This Act, intended to secure fixity of tenure and fair rent to the tenant and to promote cordiality in relationship between the landlord and the tenant where land is leased for cultivation, the lessee gives the owner of the land, 50 per cent of the produce.

Under the Act the tenancy of any land can be terminated only on the following grounds :

(1) The tenants default in the payment of rent for any year;
(2) Any act done by the tenant which is destructive or injurious to the land;
(3) Sub-division or sub-letting of the land;
(4) The tenants negligence by allowing the land to remain fallow; and
(5) The use of land for purposes unrelated to agriculture.[8]

The Karnataka Land Reforms Act which came into effect in 1965 was amended in 1974 and was implemented. According to this Act, right of ownership of land was granted to landlords on the condition that they bear any of the labour, or risks of cultivation. All tenancies were abolished and the existing leases were abrogated. The right of resumption of land by the owner was completely prohibited. However, the tenancy laws are not according to the prescriptions given by the Central Government in 1972 to the state.

Another change brought about by this law was that the privilege of owning land for personal cultivation was given to a very restricted class of institutions and organisations like the co-operatives and companies. Persons with non-agricultural annual income of more than Rs. 1000 were restricted from acquiring agricultural lands. The Act further provided for introduction of the constitution of Land Tribunals with non-official participation.

---

8. Malaviya, H. V. (1954), *Land Reforms in India,* Calcutta, Sri Gouranga Press, p. 45.

To begin with 192 land tribunals were set up in the 175 taluks of the State. Thus, there is atleast one tribunal for each taluk. The non-official members in the Tribunal include, one member from the SC and ST communities. All the others are also drawn locally. The non-officials will contribute knowledge of local conditions and practices to the deliberations of the tribunals.

Tenancy has been abolished by the declaration that all tenanted lands vested with the Government on the appointed date and that ownership thereon will be granted to the tenant-cultivator whose eligibility is enquired into by the tribunal on an application. The tribunal has to decide as to whom ownership could be given. The government further made enquiries to check whether the tenants are aware of their right and have filed in applications. It was found that there was shortfall in the number of applications. The tribunals were asked to continue to accept applications. This went on till June, 1977.

During January 1979, some more amendments were introduced of which two have some special significance. First, the date for filing applications was extended till 30th June, 1979. Secondly the agricultural labourers having homesteads on the agricultural land owned by someone else were given the facility to obtain ownership of the dwelling house and the site around it by application to the tribunal.

Each tenancy application and surplus declaration demands a good lot of work. Notices are to be issued to parties concerned, filed reports are to be obtained, written statements of the parties are to be filed, extracts from the revenue records should be taken, records of oral evidence have to be made, tribunal decisions have to be communicated and collection of applications from intending allottees and so on.

It was estimated that at the end of June, 1979 there were 8 lakh applications pending before the tribunals in the State.

While studying the land reforms in the State, some important factors have to be considered. The State had different political systems hardly 50 years back. The administrative base for carrying out the land reforms programme had distinct variations in different areas of Karnataka. The State was reorganised 25 years ago. The merging of all the sub-systems of administrations was complex. We can take the case of South Kanara as an example. This district was formerly part of Madras Presidency under the British. The right, promulgated in 1964 under a new unified Land Revenue Act had not been fully introduced even by 1974.[9]

The survey department had not changed by 1974 to the 'Hissa' survey system prevalent in the rest of the State. This district which had the largest incidence of tenancy, thus, had also the largest gap in updating of land-records pertaining to tenancy. Some districts viz., Gulbarga, Bijapur, Bidar and Bellary had heavy concentration of holdings in the size group of 30 hectares and above. From all these we come to know, that the impact of the Act, will not be uniform throughout the State.

On the basis of the data supplied by the informants, an attempt was made to evaluate the land reforms in Karnataka. In this study it has been found throughout that almost all the rural houseless have been invariably landless.

Out of the total 2924 respondents, 2636 (90.1 per cent) have said that they did not know about the land reforms. Only 230 (7.8 per cent) respondents are aware of the recent changes regarding land-holding pattern and the remaining are totally ignorant of this scheme.

The Karnataka Land Reforms Act, is said to be one of the progressive piece of land legislation. But the Act cannot become a progressive one, until the people have a thorough knowledge about it. Whether t heAct produced the desired changes or not, the first thing required is that the people should be educated about the land reforms in such a way that they should begin to view this in right perspective.

The land reforms did not have any impact on the landless because their socio-economic conditions remain unchanged

9. Rajan, M. A. S., (1979), Implementation of Land Reforms—The Karnataka Experience 39th Annual Conference of the Indian Society of Agricultural Economics.

inspite of implementation of land-reforms. Out of 2924 respondents (97.7 per cent) have given a negative answer regarding the land-distribution among the landless farmers in the respective villages.

It has been observed that only a minority *i.e.*, 16 respondents affirmed that there is equal land-distribution among the landless farmers in the villages. About 31 (1.1 per cent) respondents have not responded to this question and 21 (0.7 per cent) have answered that they did not have any idea regarding this.

Though majority in the sample have stated that they are not aware of the recent changes in the land-holding pattern, nearly 15 per cent admitted that they are affected by the new land-laws.

While 229 (7.8 per cent) families are benefitted by the scheme, some 194 families said, they have lost landed property under the scheme. It is true some landless families were given lands by the government under various schemes, generally SC/ST families come under this category. The families who have lost are by and large, non-cultivators and widows. The law has not provided any exception for widows to keep lands though they are not actual cultivators, Table 29.

Nevertheless, half the sample households have indicated that all village residents must own lands; refer Table 30.

As explained in the earlier chapters land is an economic commodity upon which majority depend. It is also a source to attain social status. Therefore, naturally village people feel that they should own some land which gives them economic security and social standing. However, the fact, 47 per cent respondents have mentioned that it is not necessary to own land is something revealing. Perhaps being landless they have had the experience of possessing uneconomic holding. Mere ownership of one or two acres of dry land, that too far away from the village, more than being an economic security has been a source of loss to them. If they are not having the bullock and agricultural implements, such lands are a real burden.

About 54 per cent respondents have started that everyone can become a successful cultivator. What is essential to them is land along with certain monetary assistance. According to them Indian

TABLE 29

Land Reforms—Have you been Affected by the New Scheme ?

Sl. No.	Name of the District	Benefitted	Put to loss	No Response	Not applicable	Total
1.	Bangalore	23	14	313	—	350
2.	Chikmagalur	16	11	201	—	228
3.	Chitradurga	11	13	235	2	261
4.	Coorg	4	3	112	2	121
5.	Hassan	25	16	189	2	232
6.	Kolar	29	14	282	24	349
7.	Mandya	12	62	166	1	241
8.	Mysore	30	19	213	42	304
9.	Shimoga	47	13	230	10	300
10.	South Kanara	15	15	205	6	241
11.	Tumkur	17	14	263	3	297
	Total	229	194	2409	92	2924
	Percentage	7.8	6.6	82.3	3.1	

TABLE 30

Do you think all villagers must own land ?

Sl. No.	*Name of the District*	*Yes*	*No*	*No Response*	*No Opinion*	*Total*
1.	Bangalore	—	349	1	—	350
2.	Chikmagalur	110	110	1	7	228
3.	Chitradurga	—	257	2	2	261
4.	Coorg	73	40	6	2	121
5.	Hassan	108	121	2	1	232
6.	Kolar	343	3	1	2	349
7.	Mandya	236	4	1	0	241
8.	Mysore	120	182	—	2	304
9.	Shimoga	92	208	—	—	300
10.	South Kanara	131	106	4	—	241
11.	Tumkur	292	—	4	1	297
	Total	1505	1380	22	17	2924
	Percentage	51.4	47.1	0.7	0.5	

agriculture does not require any special technical skill. Their experience with nature and land is to grow enough products required for their living. In fact, they have learnt so-called modern method of cultivation as they are working on other land, doing all these every season. Hence in their opinion everyone can become a successful cultivator. But nearly 45.3 per cent sample households have negated this proposition. For them more possession of land is not enough. One should have other facilities like bullock-carts, manure and other basic agricultural implements. Even though they are aware of the method of cultivation, it is not sufficient to succeed in agriculture. The rural landless agricultural labourers are poor and hence cannot prosper as cultivators.

Nearly 57 per cent of the respondents are in favour of land-reforms. They said that government should help the rural poor by implementing such measures effectively. Among those who supported such measures, majority are in favour of continuing these schemes for about ten years. Only 2.7 per cent require the measures to be extended for twenty years, refer Table 31.

Regarding land-tribunals 95.2 per cent are aware of such bodies. Effectively after 1974, the State Government has hastened the land reforms and set up atleast one land tribunal in each taluk. The news has reached many villages because it affects the villagers' social and economic life. It is possible that some of the respondents or their family-members have been parties in one or the other issues connected with tribunals. However, about 1.6 per cent have said that they are not aware of tribunals. Refer Table 32.

The respondents assessment of the land tribunals and its members were ascertained. Only 7.8 per cent have stated the tribunals are helpful. The rest have described its members as selfish and partisan (23.1 per cent). Their usual complaint was that the non-official members are biased and often work in the interest of caste and political parties. Another 13.7 per cent have criticised the working of the tribunal and its members, as corrupt. According to them the members favour those who pay money to them. They throw their weight in their favour. They have lost faith in the land-tribunals and hence, have no good opinion about this machinery, Table 33.

TABLE 31

Government must help Rural Poor through land reforms

Sl. No.	Name of the District	Yes, for Ten years	For Twenty years	For ever	Should not help	No opinion	No Response	Total
1.	Bangalore	280	7	1	—	16	46	350
2.	Chikmagalur	96	8	—	—	10	114	228
3.	Chitradurga	179	7	—	—	59	16	261
4.	Coorg	45	1	—	—	—	75	121
5.	Hassan	119	2	—	—	10	101	232
6.	Kolar	129	9	—	—	48	163	349
7.	Mandya	97	4	—	—	37	103	241
8.	Mysore	180	12	—	—	33	79	304
9.	Shimoga	241	9	—	—	25	25	300
10.	South Kanara	109	11	—	—	17	104	241
11.	Tumkur	121	10	—	—	29	137	297
	Total	1596	80	1	—	284	963	2924
	Percentage	54.5	2.7	0.03	—	9.7	32.9	

TABLE 32

Are you aware of Land Tribunals ?

Sl. No.	Name of the District	Yes	No	No Response	Not Applicable	Total
1.	Bangalore	349	1	—	—	350
2.	Chikmagalur	225	3	—	—	228
3.	Chitradurga	252	7	2	—	261
4.	Coorg	110	9	2	—	121
5.	Hassan	226	4	2	—	232
6.	Kolar	323	2	24	—	349
7.	Mandya	238	2	1	—	241
8.	Mysore	261	1	42	—	304
9.	Shimoga	282	8	10	—	300
10.	South Kanara	226	9	6	—	241
11.	Tumkur	292	2	3	—	297
	Total	2784	48	92	—	2924
	Percentage	95.2	1.6	3.1		

TABLE 33

Opinion about the Role of Land Tribunals

Sl. No.	Name of the District	Helpful	Selfish	Partisan	Corrupt	No Response	Total
1.	Bangalore	23	95	205	27	—	350
2.	Chikmagalur	16	88	112	12	—	228
3.	Chitradurga	11	75	125	48	2	261
4.	Coorg	4	34	66	15	2	121
5.	Hassan	25	49	101	55	2	232
6.	Kolar	29	54	196	46	24	349
7.	Mandya	12	42	108	78	1	241
8.	Mysore	30	52	148	32	42	304
9.	Shimoga	47	39	161	43	10	300
10.	South Kanara	15	82	118	20	6	241
11.	Tumkur	17	68	182	27	3	297
	Total	229	678	1522	403	92	2924
	Percentage	7.8	23.1	52.0	13.7	3.1	

Majority of the respondents think that the land tribunals cannot resolve the disputes satisfactorily. Since most of them have said that the members of the tribunals are partisan, selfish and corrupt, it is but natural that they do not trust them.

As many as 38.5 per cent respondents are not sure whether the land tribunals resolve the disputes objectively. Only 11.0 per cent have answered positively. However, 21.5 per cent have indicated that if the tribunals consist of only official members they can discharge the duties of the tribunal and resolve land-disputes satisfactorily. According to them the source of all problems of tribunals are the non-official members.

In view of the complex nature of the land relationships in rural areas, it is desirable to evaluate the success or otherwise of the land reforms particularly land-ceiling policy. Firstly the ceiling on land-holdings is not possible in the irrigated areas because the landlords normally divide their property among their relatives and friends or adopt such devices that each of the newly created holdings fall below the proposed maximum. For this process, the expression 'paper partitions' is used.

After enforcing land-ceiling laws only very little or negligible area is likely to be available for redistribution to landless labourers and uneconomic holders or small farmers. The ceiling is likely to be frustrating in most cases and would lead to land-concentration because in majority of the cases land has been either distributed or transferred among the family-members or relatives and each of them has got just the economic holdings or below the ceiling limit.

Land reforms in Karnataka is considered to be effective in the sense that a minority section of rural landless have got a few acres—say one or two acres—of land. But the problem is that usually these are barren lands. This land is not going to improve the condition of the rural landless in any way. Even when cultivable land is given, his position still remains poor. Since, daily life itself poses a problem to the farmer, he is not in a position to purchase new implements or have good bullock or instal a pumpset or a tube-well.

Co-operatives have not made the desired impact on the life of the rural people, much less on the weaker sections of the population. Huge subsidy provided have either been squandered or mismanaged by the corrupt office bearers. The poor and the landless have not been benefitted much by this institution.

About 36 per cent households, in the sample are members of the co-operative societies in the village. A large majority, however, are not members. Since the membership is given only to the shareholders, many poor cannot become members and utilise the benefits provided. Due to illiteracy and ignorance the villagers cannot understand the spirit of co-operation and therefore the movement is not a success in many states.

A large number of members have said that they purchase only essential commodities. A small number (38 families) have purchased agricultural implements through the co-operative societies. Another 47 respondents have drawn loans from the society.

Fractional fights and favouritism are rampant in the village co-operative societies. Huge sums of loan are outstanding without being recovered. Government has stopped assistance to such institutions so the spirit of self help and community good have almost disappeared from the rural scene. If the recent trends are any indication, the co-operatives have no future in our rural society.

All is not well with the village Panchayats. These institutions of local self-government are being dominated by the rich agricultural castes. Since most of the development schemes are implemented through panchayats interested parties are cornering all the benefits. The poor are not cared.

Only 6.1 per cent respondents have said that either they or their family members are members of the Panchayat. Nearly 60 per cent are not members. Only 1.2 per cent respondents have mentioned that their caste Panchayat members are working as Chairmen. While 16 persons are holding the office as Vice-Chairman, four are associated in the capacity as secretary. About 107 households have ordinary members in the Panchayat.

By and large, Panchayats are ridden with factionalism, followed by caste-politics. Only a small number of respondents have stated, they are playing useful role, refer Table 34.

About 83.8 per cent families in the sample say that the Panchayats work in favour of only a few vocal villagers who have dominated the Panchayats for number of years. Nearly 10.6 per cent say Panchayats as useless.

The above assessment of Panchayats by respondents is a clear indication how these democratic institutions are shaping.

Though the co-operatives are set up with the intension of giving loans to cultivators, they did not make much progress due to lack of support by the government, illiteracy of members, lack of co-operative spirit among village leaders, and dishonesty of managing committee members.

The role of village Panchayats regarding the implementation of land reforms is also not satisfactory. The Panchayats are dominated by upper castes and rich land owners who have a vested interest and pay lip service to legislation. Even when the Panchayat consists of people from other sections, they are also often under the influence of all powerful big landlords and in this way Panchayats fail to inspire confidence among the majority of peasants. The interest of small minority are served at the cost of needy majority. Thus we find that the land-reforms have not reached the rural landless because of these impediments.

Usually laws are intended for achieving some effects in the economic or social sphere within the state. Whereas in land-reforms, a strong element of equality is found in their desired changes. Land reform laws produce some social and political effects as soon as it is implemented. Sometimes, the very threat of law may produce effects. In almost all states Politics colours the land-reforms.

From the agriculturists point of view, the impact of land-reforms is indirect in nature. M.A.S. Rajan has given two reasons for this 'In the first place, for the cultivator and the landless, the land-reforms programme is just like any other government oriented programmes. The law has laid down certain procedures. It expects certain results to follow. Many legislative programmes

TABLE 34

Opinion about the Role of Panchayat

Sl. No.	*Name of the District*	*Useful*	*Factiona-lism*	*Caste Politics*	*Favouri-tism*	*Useless*	*No Response*	*Total*
1.	Bangalore	8	206	68	40	26	2	350
2.	Chikmagalur	12	94	59	30	31	2	228
3.	Chitradurga	10	134	60	24	29	4	261
4.	Coorg	7	43	30	21	19	1	121
5.	Hassan	14	96	70	19	28	5	232
6.	Kolar	19	184	84	23	36	3	349
7.	Mandya	11	104	78	27	19	2	241
8.	Mysore	9	135	93	31	30	6	304
9.	Shimoga	10	148	100	16	25	1	300
10.	South Kanara	7	92	75	25	40	2	241
11.	Tumkur	16	133	80	33	27	8	297
	Total	123	1369	797	289	310	36	2924
	Percentage	4.2	46.8	27.2	9.8	10.6	1.2	

which made similar demands have come and gone in the rural areas. The more powerful people have coped with these programmes either to secure benefits or avoid a disadvantage of the state. But the game is played everywhere, and it is rather serious.

In the second place, land is very much part of a system of transactions. Land is not a rationed commodity. Within certain bonds it can be freely transacted and transactions do take place. . . lands are sold and bought for a variety of reasons both monetary and non-monetary transactions, by sale, by exchange, by partition and settlement, by gift or mortgage. . . . but not on lease any more. Many of these transactions are left unregistered. They are based on mere faith and oral agreement. When some disputes occur, they are settled informally by local panchayat leaders and elders or else parties go to the courts. The total number of operational holdings in the state is estimated at 35 to 45 lakhs. Land holdings are likely to be strongly influenced by the land market rather than by any direct action under a law like the Land Reforms Act.[10]

10. Rajan, M.A.S. (1979), Implementation of Land Reforms—The Karnataka Experience. 39th Annual Conference of the Indian Society of Agricultural Economics.

8

Concluding Remarks

IN THE following pages some of the important problems connected with housing which have already been discussed earlier will be highlighted, and some suggestions to meet the contingencies would be offered.

Shelter, like food and clothing is one of the essential requirements for human existence. But unfortunately quite a large section of people all over the world, in India as well as in Karnataka run short of meeting these essential requirements.

Housing can be further looked at as the most basic requirement without which living would be terribly uncomfortable. In the Indian setting, the vagaries of the climatic conditions, poverty and allied problems have made a number of people to live under such sub-standard conditions. The pavement dwellers found in thousands in all our big cities and towns, the innumerable and overcrowded slums where people live under conditions and physical surroundings unfit even for animals are, cases in point.

Houseless often goes with poverty and these together would not only affect the physical but also social environment. Many social evils and health problems can be traced to such environment.

As against the city and town situations, the Indian villages provide a unique picture of human settlements which houses not only human beings but also draught animals and all other possible things. It is true slum conditions and pavement-dwellers are absent in villages. But the houses, themselves in a large number of cases particularly of the poorer sections are really sub-standard dwelling units.

Housing has always been a continuous problem. It cannot cope up with the increasing population and their mobility. Like Indian agriculture, Indian joint-family households are also subjected to much division and fragmentation apart from overcrowding. In the backdrop of this, the number of houseless people have emerged as a category in rural India and Karnataka.

Over the years, the welfare policies adopted by the governments; at the centre and the state level, housing is also included. The governments housing provisions have been discussed at some length in Chapters II and III which suggests the enormity of the problem particularly in villages. It may be recalled that :

> "In 1971 there were about 9.3 crores dwelling units in India in which 10.5 crore households lived. Out of these about 8.1 crores housing units were considered usable 'pucca', 'semi-pucca' and 'serviceable kachcha' houses. The shortage worked out to be 2.4 crore dwelling units. This accounted for 0.55 crore in urban areas and 1.85 crores in rural areas. Further, the annual shortage is estimated at 20 lakh units due to the growth of population."

Right from first five year plan to the end of fourth five year plan, housing was allotted a decreasing percentage of resources starting with 18 per cent, it came down to 4 per cent. In the meantime, several housing schemes were introduced. They are :

1. Integrated subsidised housing scheme for industrial workers and economically weaker sections ;
2. Low income group housing scheme ;
3. Subsidised housing scheme for plantation workers ;
4. Slum clearance and improvement scheme ;
5. Village housing project scheme ;
6. Middle income group housing scheme ;
7. Rental housing scheme for state government employees ;

Four important organisations connected with housing have emerged over the years. They are :

1. National Building Organisations (NBO) ;
2. National Buildings Construction Corporation Limited (NBCC) ;
3. Housing and Urban Development Corporation (HUDCO);
4. Hindustan Housing Factory (HHF).

These organisations have a network covering all the states in the country including Karnataka.

Out of the five broad natural regions in Karnataka Coastal, Malnad, Semi-Malnad Southern Maidan and Northern Maidan, excepting the last, the other four regions are included in the present study. There are regional variations in the location of villages and type of houses. A variety of structures using different materials can be found as one goes through the different regions of the state.

The differentiation between the *kachcha* and *pucca* occurs among houses only on the basis of kind of materials that are used to construct the house. The major distinctions between the two, however, is that *kachcha* houses are built with non-durable materials, whereas the *pucca* houses are built with durable materials having long life expectancy. The poor and the houseless in rural Karnataka have small huts built from non-durable materials which are easily perishable as they are usually mud-constructions with thatched roofs. Chapter III contains detailed information in this connection.

The economic conditions of the people living in *kachcha* houses and houseless peoples more or less, tally. They face problems of both economic and physical insecurity.

The State Government like the Centre has also embarked upon a programme of action in connection with housing both in urban and rural areas. In the present study, attention is focussed on the rural scheme which are discussed in the body of the report in detail.

Chapters IV to VII covers the empirical data relating to the

Revenue Divisions which include eleven out of nineteen districts in the state.

Chapter IV focussed on the background of rural houseless in Karnataka. Many villagers consider that there is dearth of houses and people must have a house to feel secure. Those who are without a house are facing this problem for a number of years. Majority of the houseless live with relatives and a good number are under the mercy of rural landlords. While they are aware of governmental schemes for the welfare of houseless, many have not availed these benefits. They consider that the government-scheme is good and the role of Panchayat is helpful.

Chapter V deals with the socio-economic conditions of the rural houseless poor, the landless and those living in *Janata* houses, type of occupation, duration of employment, income and material possession. The social life, and hygienic habits are considered.

Majority of the houseless are landless agricultural labourers. Many are under-employed and get work for less 6 months in a year. Usually all adult members and children in the family work to supplement family income. Wages are very low and earnings are meagre. The minimum wages for agricultural labour has not been enforced. Large number of houseless do not own any land. Hardly they have other assets like cattle, sheep, poultry. Their social and cultural life is not different from others in the village.

Chapter VI gives details of planned housing in Karnataka. The State is considered to be in the forefront in implementing schemes for rural houseless. Till the end of August 1978 about 1.44 lakh houses were constructed in rural areas. About 7.87 lakh house-sites have been distributed during the period 1972-1978. A sum of about Rs. 2 crores were spent during 1977-1979.

Persons from all caste and religions are given *Janata* houses. The houses are small and the average number of persons living is five. The space in the *Janata* houses is not sufficient. One of the conditions of allotment is that the houses cannot be alienated, sold or exchanged. But many feel they can sell, transfer and mortgage the houses. The houses are not having many basic amenities like proper approach roads, electricity, water and sanitation.

Finally, details of land Reforms in the State and its relevance to the rural houseless have been discussed in Chapter VII. Karnataka has been declared as the pioneer state in which land reforms have been effectively enforced.

Co-operatives and Panchayats have not helped the rural poor. Panchayats, they say, work in favour of only a few vocal villagers.

The data bears that majority of the landless are also houseless and *vice versa.*

To effectively tackle the housing problems in rural Karnataka, the following few suggestions are offered.

Suggestions

1. The rural poor are also landless and houseless. Details of their economic, social and living conditions are not available. The census data does not reflect local and regional differences. Therefore, efforts must be made to locate the poor and know their socio-economic conditions.

   A national register should be opened to include all details of economic social and housing particulars of each family living in rural and urban areas of the country. An agency at the national and state level should be entrusted with the task of enumeration.

   Based on the details available in the national register, it would be possible for planning various schemes for the welfare of the poor and the houseless.

2. Priority should be given to provide house-sites or houses to poor people in the villages by utilising lands acquired under the land-reforms scheme. In the southern and northern maidan districts of the state lands acquired adjacent to the villages should be used for this purpose. In the coastal districts and malnad areas, landless and houseless families may be encouraged to settle on agricultural lands allotted to them under the scheme.

3. While allotting house-sites and houses to rural poor it should be ensured that poor people from all caste groups and religions are given their houses to form a mixed housing colony. Segregation of caste and religious groups should be avoided.
4. The problem of houseless and site-less can never be solved so long they are given personal ownership. To avoid mortgage, sale and further sub-division, rights to reside may be conferred on the beneficiaries as against private ownership which is always vulnerable and the problem of houseless will continue to persist endlessly.
5. As far as possible house-sites and houses to the houseless and poor in rural areas should be provided in the vicinity of the main village.
6. Those who have house-sites and are in need of government assistance to build their own house should be encouraged to construct houses by using locally available building materials.

   If the beneficiaries are given governmental assistance like wooden doors and windows, tiles, palm thatch and other building materials, it must be ensured, scrutinised and certified that the quality and quantity of materials are actually used in the construction. Any abuse of these assistance established, the concerned should be penalised.
7. The present practice of identifying beneficiaries and working out schemes for the benefit of the poor and the houseless by the village Panchayats and the Block Development Officer should be discontinued. Because of corruption, nepotism, and casteism, the benefits of welfare schemes are not reaching the really needy. A separate agency at the national level stretching to village level should be set up.
8. Construction work of *Janata* houses should not be entrusted to private contractors in the villages. Instead voluntary organisations should be requested to take up such assignments. The Land Army can be considered.

9. Facilities like approach roads, electricity and drinking water-wells should be provided to *Janata* housing colonies in the villages.
10. All major and minor civil work should be carried out under government control. The present practice of giving contracts should be discontinued.
11. To improve the economic condition of agricultural and casual labourers, all kind of labour contracts should be stopped. Construction and repair of roads, tanks and canals should not be entrusted to private contractors. A separate agency at the state level should be set up for executing such works.
12. In the case of attached farm labourers the new law confers on them, rights of ownership of farm-houses in which they are now living. The landlords create a lot of problems to such poor labourers. Therefore, the scope of new laws should include provisions to assess the cost of the farm house and land in which the attached labourers are residing. The assessed amount should be recovered from the land-lords by the government. Alternative housing accommodation should be given to them by utilising the money recovered and if necessary by providing special assistance through subsidies.
13. Minimum Wages Act of 1948 should be strictly enforced to cover all kind of labourers. Wages should be linked to the cost of living and it should be periodically revised.
14. The poor and jobless should be encouraged to migrate to places of major river valley projects and mining sites in the state. In such places, employers should provide basic needs like house, health and education facilities to all workers working with them.
15. Medium and small scale industries should be encouraged and started in rural areas. These will help absorb additional and surplus labour in villages.
16. The National Building Organisation should expand its activities to States and set up research wings to work on

rural housing and other necessities.

17. As regards the financial requirements we have to evolve some definite and practicable solution to meet the investment out of the meagre savings.
18. Co-ordinated efforts will have to be made to bring together the scientific and technological innovations in the country for exploitation and use of the available scarce house building material resources.
19. We should know what housing materials are needed? How much investment is needed for these materials? Social values and local expertise can be of great help in assessing these requirements.
20. Curriculum in the educational institutions at all levels should include subjects connected with rural problems and provisions as may be highlighted from readily available empirical studies.
21. Rural service for a specified period should be made compulsory for every college student before he gets his graduation.

Bibliography

Abrams, C., *The future of housing*, New York, Harper and Bros., 1946.

——: *Housing in the Modern World*, London, Faber and Faber, 1964.

Alum, J. and Dr. Ing., *Low cost housing for rural areas*, Dacca, 1970.

American Public Health Association, "Planning the home occupancy", Chicago Public Administration Service, 1950.

Bemis, E. C. and John Burchard, *The Evolving house : A History of the Home*; Vol. 1, Cambridge, Mass : The Technology Press, M. I. T., 1933.

Beyer, Thomas, W., Mackersey and James E. Montgomery, *Houses are for people*, Research Publication No 3, Ithaca, N. Y. : Cornell University Housing Research Centre, 1955.

Bayer, Glenn, H. : *Housing and Personal Values*, Memoir 364, Ithaca, N. Y. : Cornell Univerity, Agricultural Experiment Station, July, 1959.

——: *Housing and Society*, New York, Macmillan Co., 1965.

Beyer, G. H. and J. Hugh Rose, *Farm Housing*, A volume in the census monograph series, New York, John Wiley and Sons, 1957.

Bhaskara Rao, B. : *Housing 2000 A. D.—A long perspective for India*, Operations Research Group, Baroda, 1975.

Census of India 1961, Vol. 1. Part IV-A (iii) Report on House types and village settlement patterns in India.

—— 1971, Series 14, Mysore Part I V, Report on Housing.

—— 1971, Series 14, Mysore, Part II A General population tables.

—— 1971, Series I, Part IV-B, Housing tables.

S. K. Chandhoke, "Housing Conditions in Rural India", *I.C.C. Quarterly*, Vol. 4, No. 2, 1977, pp. 172-183.

Charles M. Correa, "Third world housing : space as a resource", *Ekistics*, 34:242, Jan., 1976.

Commission on Race and Housing : *Where shall we live*? Berkeley, University of California Press, 1958.

Cutler Virginia, F., "Personal and family values in the choice of a home", *Ithaca*, N. Y. : Cornell University Agricultural experiment station Bulletin 840, November, 1947.

Dean, J. P., *Home ownership; Is it sound* ? New York : Harper and Bros., 1945.

Deutsch, Morton and Mary Evant Collins, *Interracial Housing—A Psychological Evaluation of Social Experiment*, Menneapolis, University of Minnesota Press, 1951.

Dosiadis, C.A., *The human settlements that we need*, New Delhi, Tata McGraw Hill Pub. Co. Ltd., 1976.

Faulkener, Ray, *Inside Today's Home*, New York; Holt Rinehart and Winston, 1960.

Foote, Nelson, N. *et. al*, *Housing choices and housing constraints*, New York, McGraw Hill Book Co., 1960.

Glazer, Nathan and Davis McEntire (eds.), *Studies in Housing and Minority Groups*, Berkeley : University of California Press, 1960.

Government of India : *Housing the People*, New Delhi, Publications Division, Ministry of Information and Broadcasting, 1975.

Grebler, Leo, *Production of New housing*; New York, Social Science Research Council, 1950.

Gries, John, M. and James Ford (eds.), *Home Ownership, Income and Types of Dwelling*, Vol. IV, The President's Conference on Home Building and Home Ownership, Washington D.C., 1932.

Grimes F, Oruille, *Housing for low-income urban families*, Baltimore, John Hopkins University Press, 1976.

Haque, N., *Development of Extra-thin shell for cheap housing*, The problem of the common man, Agricultural University, 1969.

Hartman, W. C., *Housing and social policy*, Prentice Hall Inc., U.S.A., 1975.

HUDCO, "Objectives and Achievements," Pamphlet, New Delhi, 1971.

Isler, M. L., *Thinking about housing*, Washington, D. C., The Urban Institution, 1970.

John, F. C. Turner, "Housing issues and the standards problem", *Ekistics*, 152, 196, March, 1972.

——, "Approach to government sponsored housing", *Ekistics*, 4, 242, January, 1976.

Jain, J. P., Chandra, Mahesh and Kulshresta, R. P., Fire retardant treatment of the Thatch", *C.B.R.I., Technical Note*, August, 1976.

Jain S. C., *Agricultural Policy in India*, Delhi, Allied Publishers Ltd., 1967.

Kelly, Burnham, *The Pre-fabrication of house*, New York, Technology Press of Massachusetts Institute of Technology and John Wiley and Sons, Inc., 1951.

——, *Design and production of houses*, New York, McGraw Hill Book Co., Inc., 1959.

Kennedy, R. W., *The house and the art of its design*, New York, Reinhold Publishing Corpn., 1953.

Elaber, E. H., *Housing design*, New York, Reinhold Publishing Corporation, 1954.

Leland, S., Burns and Leo Grebler, *The Housing Nations*, London, Macmillan Press Ltd., 1977.

Madan, G. R., *Indian Social Problem*, Vol. 1, New Delhi, Allied Publishers, 1976.

Maisel, Sherman, J., *House building in transition*, Berkeley : University of California Press, 1953.

Malaviya, *Land Reforms in India,* Calcutta, Sri Gauranga Press, 1954.

Mamoria, C. B., *Agricultural Problem in India*, Allahabad, Kitab Mahal, 1960.

Manickam, T. J., "Housing Crisis in the East", *Urban and Rural Planning Thought*, Vol. XIV, No, 1, Jan., 1971, pp. 1-48.

Nanavathi, M.B., and Anjaria, J.J., *Indian Rural Problem*, Bombay Indian Society of Agricultural Economics, 1970.

New Straits Times Report, Low cost housing for Pahang Tenggara Area, Kuala Lumpur, 1977.

Oktay Ural, Proceedings of the third international Symposium on lower-cost housing problems, May 1974, Montreal, Canada, Vol. 1 and Vol. 2.

Pant, S.C., *Indian Labour Problem*, Allahabad Chaitanya Publishing House, 1970.

Parvathamma, C., *Under the impact of directed changes*, New Delhi, National Publishing Co., 1978.

Parvathamma, C. and Satyanarayana, "Housing in Rural Karnataka", *University of Mysore Arts Journal*, Clo., No. XLIV, March and Sept., 1982, pp. 1-7.

——, "Housing in Rural India", *Guru Nanak Journal of Sociology*, Vol. 3 No. 2, October 1982, pp. 125-144.

Parvathamma, C., *Scheduled castes and tribes*; New Delhi, Ashish, 1984.

——, "A Stragegy for Rural Housing", Paper presented at IX World Congress of Sociology, New Delhi, August 1986.

Prakash, S. and Majumdar, N. C., "Manufacture of Bricks of improved quality." *Journal of Engineers and Planners*, 2 (8 and 9) April-June, 1974, pp. 27-30.

Rai, Mohan, Singh O. P. and Kacker, K. P.: "Door and Window frames from Magnesium Oxychloride and saw dust composition", *Research and Industry*, 16. 2, Feb., 1971, pp. 106-109.

Rangarajan, V., *Rural Housing in Tamil Nadu*, Madras, Samgam Publishers, 1976.

Readings in Co-operative Housing, Bombay, Allied Publishers, 1973.

Reid, Margaret, G., *Housing and Income*, Chicago; The University of Chicago Press, 1962.

Rene, F., Eyheralde, "Rural Housing in India", *Urban and Rural Planning Thought*, Vol. III, No. 4, October 1960, pp. 147-161.

Rogers, Kate, Ellen, *The Modern House*, U.S.A. New York; Harper and Bros., 1962.

Shah, S. M., *Rural Development Planning and Reforms*, New Delhi, Abhiman Publications, 1977.

Singh, S. M., "Wood, Wool corrugated roofing sheet", *Research and Industry*, 20 (1) March, 1975, pp. 10-11.

Singh, Y., "Role of Bamboo in Rural building construction", *Bulletin of the Builders*, Associated of India, 8 (7), July 1975, pp. 15-17.

Sinha, Bakshi, D., *Housing Growth in India*, New Delhi, Arnold Heinemann, 1976.

Sinha, I. B., "Adoption of pre-fabrication for low-income group housing" International conference on low-income housing technology and policy, A.I.T., pp. 1-15, Bangkok, June, 1977.

Souvenir, 39th Annual Conference of the Indian Society of Agricultural Economics, ISEC, Bangalore.

Stephen, H. K. Yeh and A. A. Laquian, *Housing Asia's Millions*, International Development Research Centre, Ottawa, Canada, 1979.

The YWCA of India, *A Place to live*, Bombay, Allied Publishers (P) Ltd., 1975.

Tylor Carl, C., *India's Roots of Democracy*, Bombay, Orient Longmans, 1965.

United Nations, Low cost housing in South and South-East Asia; Report of a mission of experts, New York, 1951.

——, Housing and Town and country planning Bulletin 6, "Housing in the Tropics", New York, 1952.

——, Financing of Housing and community improvement programme, New York, 1957.

——, Manual of self-help housing, New York, 1964.

——, Methods of estimating housing needs, New York, 1967.

——, Review of the housing situation in the ECAFE region, 1969.

——, Growth of the World's urban and rural population, 1900-2000, ST-SOH/Series A/44, New York, 1969.

——, A Programme of Population and Housing Censuses in countries of Asia and the far East, New York, 1970.

——, Urban and rural population; individual countries 1950-1985 and regional and major areas 1950-2000, New York, 1970.

——, World Housing Survey, report of the Secretary General, UN E/C, 6/129, New York, IV 1973.

——, Committee on Housing Building and Planning World Housing Survey, 1973.

——, Guidelines on Housing Policies for Developing Countries, New York, 1976.

——, Economic Commission for Europe; Housing for Special Groups, London, Pergaman Press, 1977.

Van Ettinger, J., *Problem and Methods of Low-income Housing* Rotterdam, 1970.

Ved Mittal, *Human Settlement Policies in the Developing Countries*, The Indian case, Institute of Social Studies, The Hague, 1977.

Violich, F., *Low-cost Housing in Latin America*, Washington, Pan American Union, 1949.

Appendix

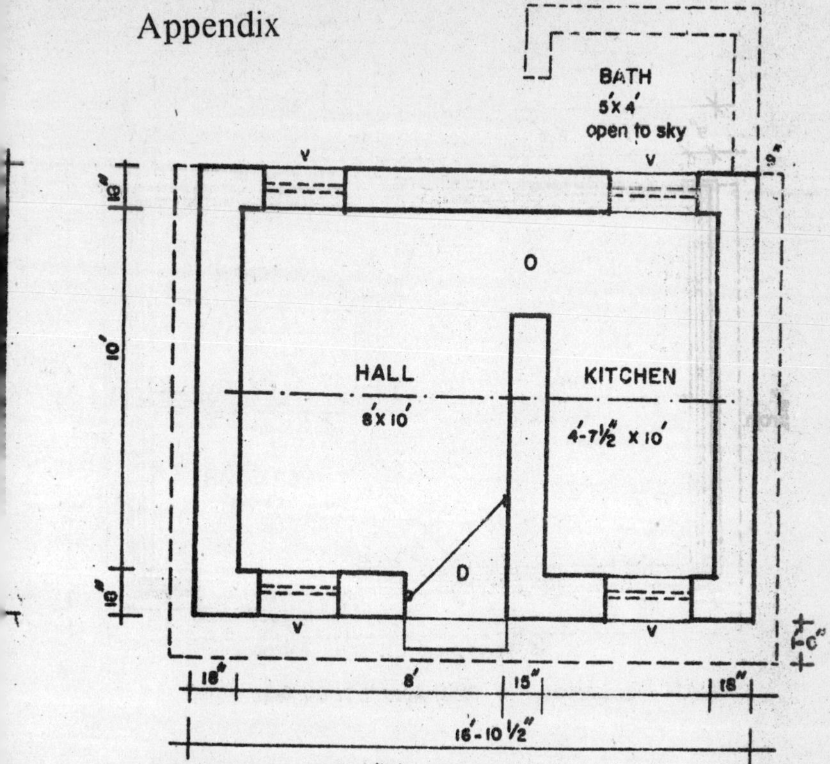

PLAN Scale: 1"= 4' Plinth Area: 220 Sq. Feet

ELEVATION

people's housing programme

18" thick mud wall and mangalore tile roofing

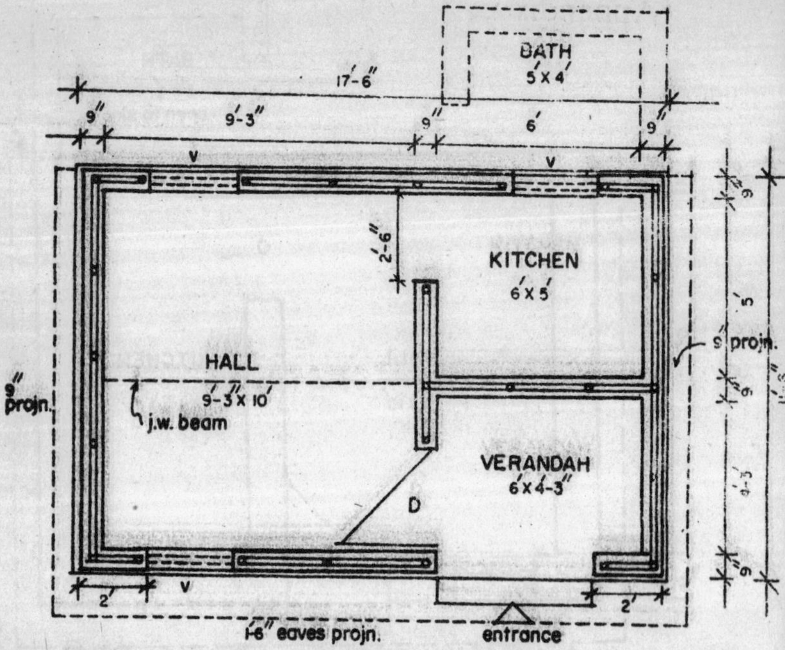

PLAN Scale: 1/4" = 1' Plinth Area: 201 Sq. Feet

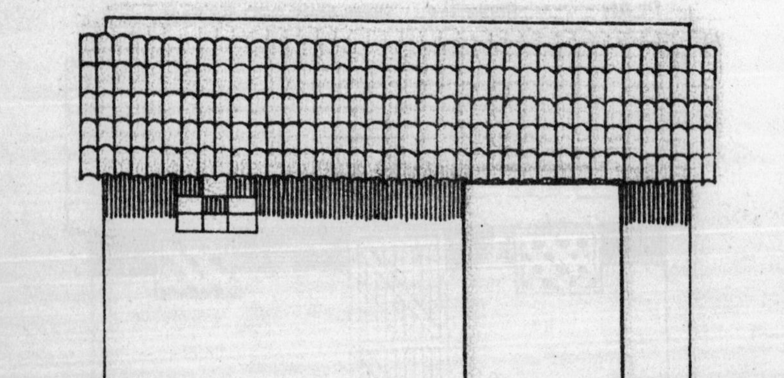

ELEVATION

people's housing programme

mud walls with split bamboo reinforcement and country tiles roofing

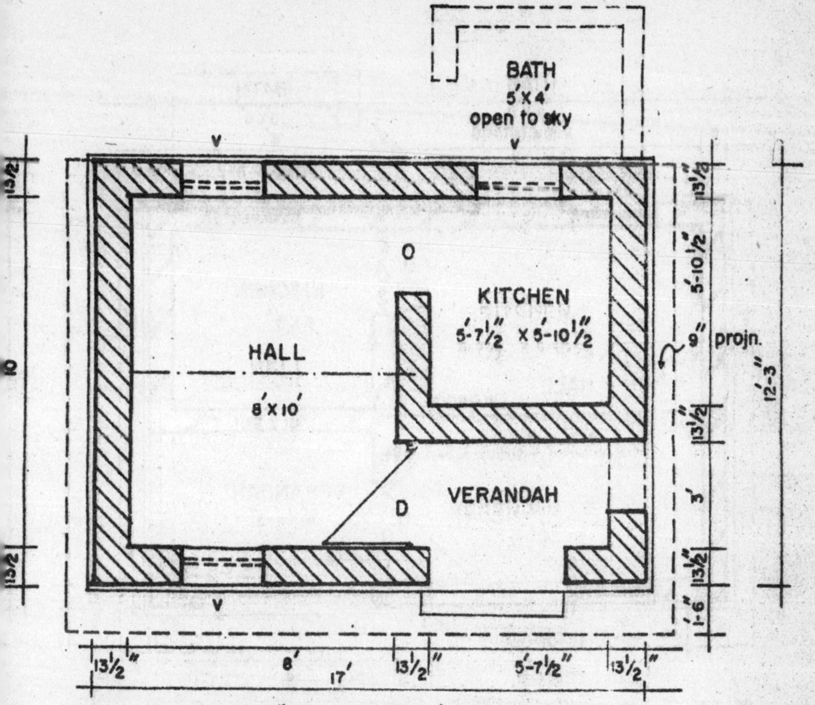

PLAN Scale: 1" = 4' Plinth Area: 208·25 Sq.Feet

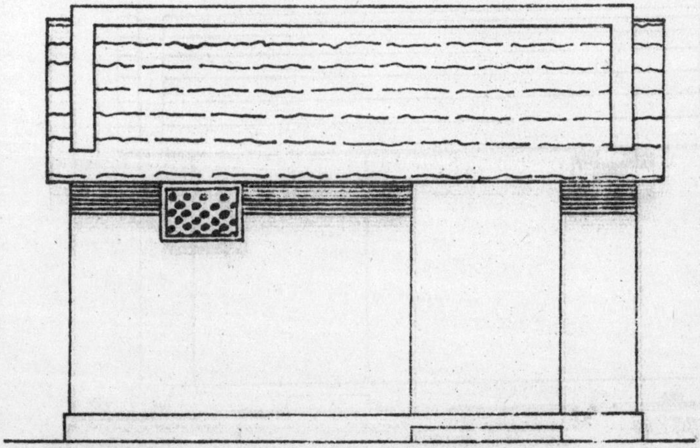

ELEVATION

people's housing programme

13 1/2" thick sundried brick wall and mangalore tile roofing

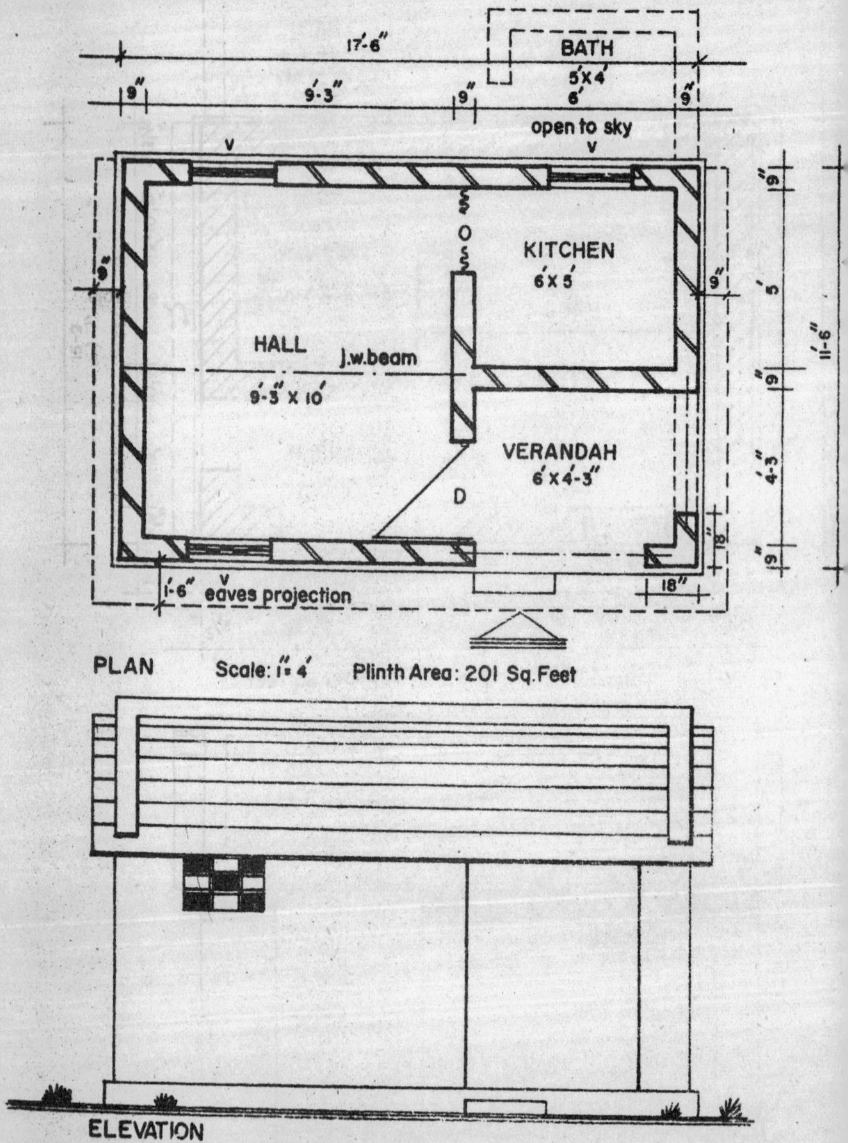

PLAN Scale: 1" = 4' Plinth Area: 201 Sq.Feet

ELEVATION

people's housing programme

burnt brick wall with mangalore tiled roofing

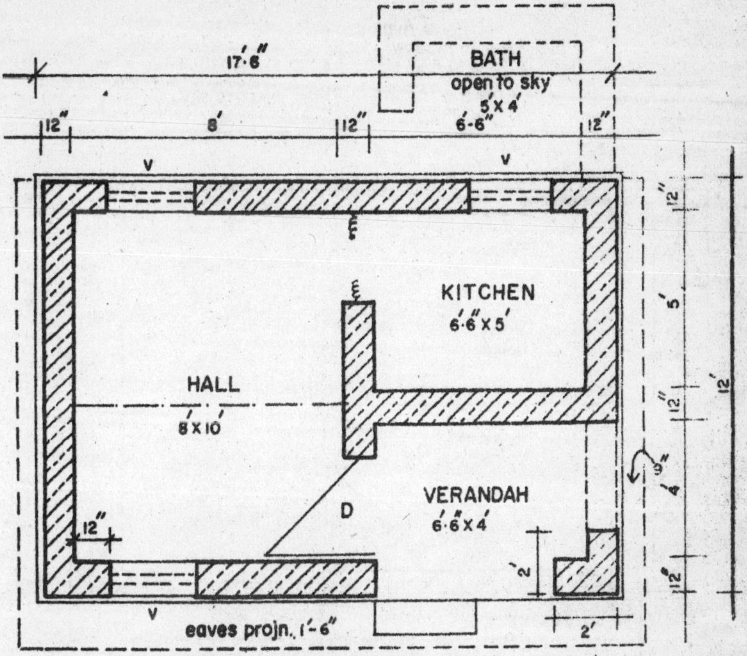

PLAN Scale: 1" = 4' Plinth Area: 210 Sq. Feet

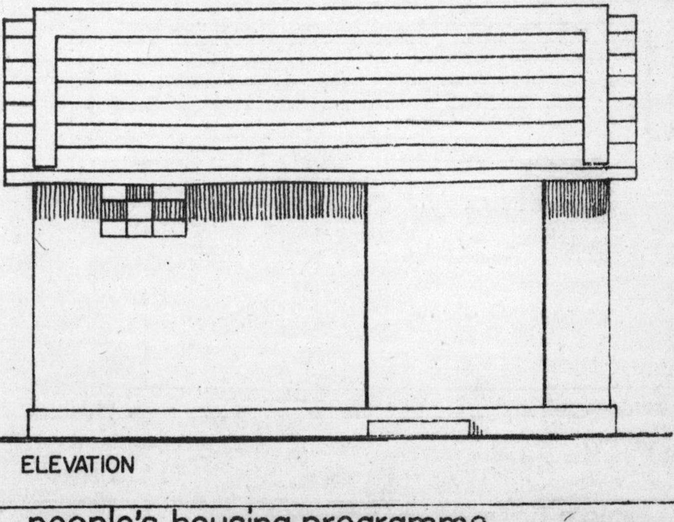

ELEVATION

people's housing programme

12" laterite wall and mangalore tile roofing

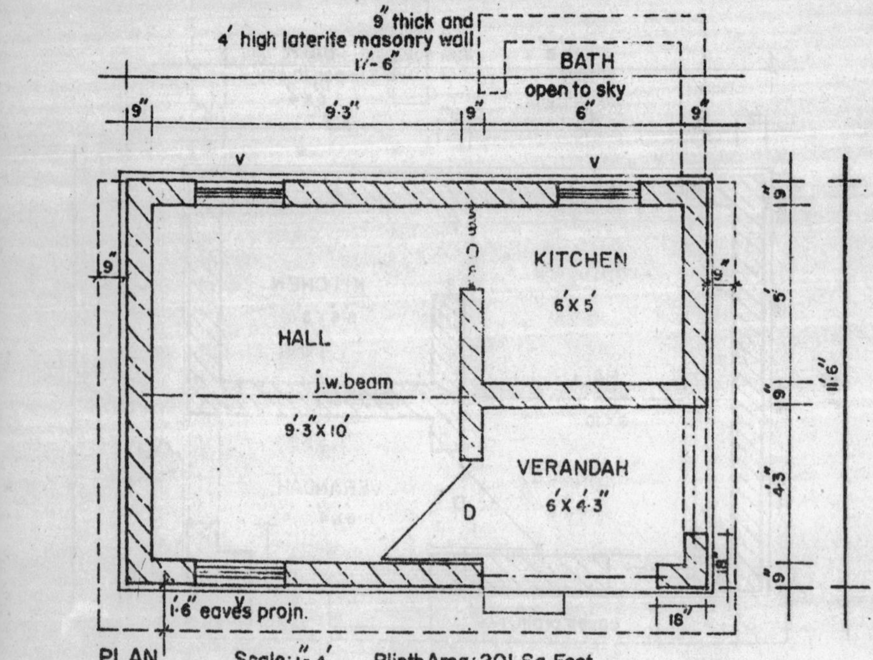

people's housing programme

9" thick laterite stone wall with mangalore tiled roofing

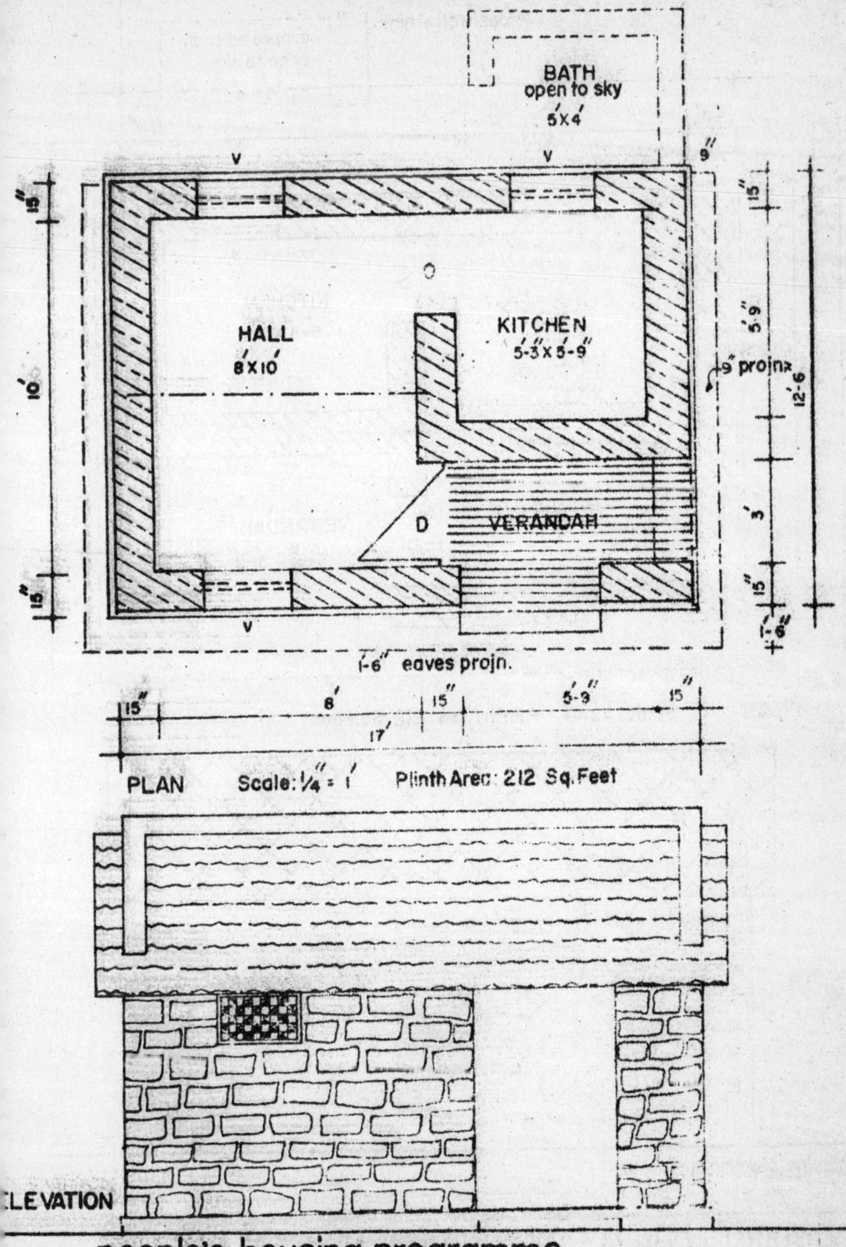

people's housing programme

15" thick r.r. masonry wall and tile roofing

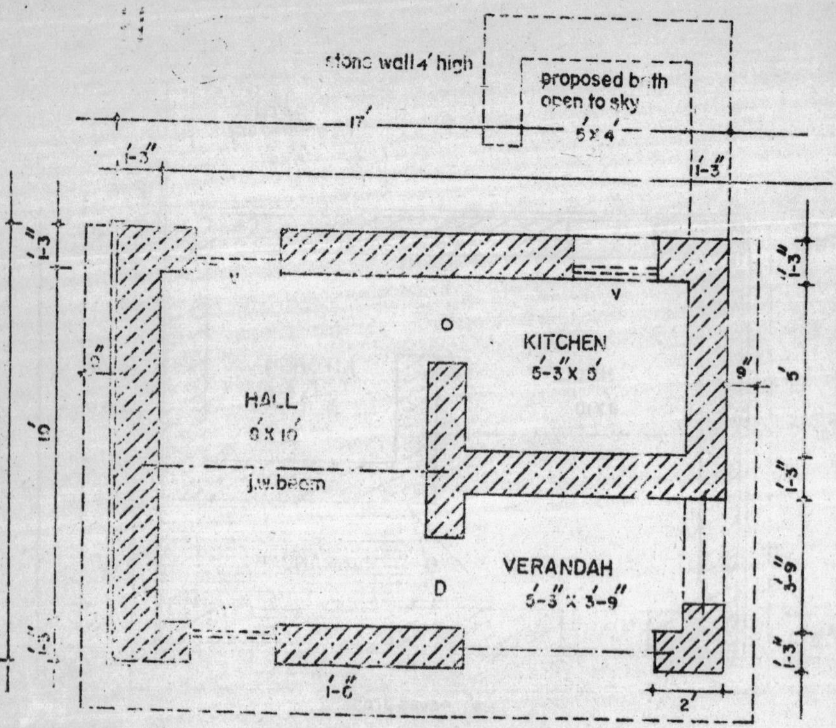

PLAN Scale: 1/4" = 1' Plinth Area: 212 Sq.Feet

ELEVATION

people's housing programme

Shahabad stone walls and roofing

Index